THANK GOD
I AM NOT VENOMOUS

THANK GOD I AM NOT VENOMOUS

CHANGE YOUR MINDSET

AASHIQ LONE

Notion Press

Old No. 38, New No. 6
McNichols Road, Chetpet
Chennai - 600 031

First Published by Notion Press 2016

ISBN 978-1-945926-08-2

Dedicated to my parents, thank you so much for making me capable of everything. And special thanks to that someone special who encouraged me every time. Love you all.

Contents

Introduction

Today if we create a new world with the same features such as flora and fauna, but without human beings, what will happen? All of us will guess, it will remain the same throughout the centuries. There would be no world war, no social crimes, no deforestation, no ozone depletion, no global warming. But when we add human beings, the whole scenario will change. The above mentioned things will start happening and there will be human hue and cry everywhere. In the former state, all living beings will live peacefully. Their nature habitat will not be changed except for a few natural disasters which is to be expected, however in the latter state everything will change. Man will ensure that no living creature can live peacefully including himself, just for the sake of his greed. Man will be responsible for extinction, and he will change the system as per his wishes.

I am not only writing this for others; if I will implement only a bit of it in myself, I can be best citizen of the world. I feel ashamed while thinking and writing about the present nature of so called human beings; we are human but sans humanity. We are only developed by technology, not developed by our thinking mind. We are so selfish and greedy that even the devil might be laughing at our deeds - to kill and destroy lives. We have kept the words like humanity, feelings, love, and affection to our dictionaries only and those words which were supposed to be kept in dictionaries are being used on daily basis like crimes, murders, rapes, domestic violence, environmental destruction, and the like. Have we once thought where humanity lives? Currently I don't think so. To be on top, we have not even spared our own family, relatives or friends. We keep murdering it on a daily basis even when we don't have time to think over it. To love somebody or being loved by someone is very rare these days. We are only carrying ego, envy, and jealousy in our mind so what can we expect at the end of the day? Look, we are not here for centuries, we are here for a limited period, say fifty to sixty years, so why should we be remembered as notorious? Why not famous after our departure? Who will change the overall mindset or thinking? No one! We should come up and think on how to change over this kind of thinking which is confined to our self only. We are human beings, we should look after the wellbeing of our planet, whether its flora, fauna, land, water or air. We should be kind to every creature in this universe. I have done some research regarding the present thinking of man, what we are carrying in our minds. All of us are not same, there are a few people who are so kind to nature and its ingredients which are being set as examples but the majority have to change our mindset towards our nature and humanity.

I am thankful to the Almighty God that he made me physically weak as compared to some heavy and big animals; if we had venom in our tongue, energy like the tiger, boldness like the lion, what could have been the result? We should have killed all living beings, I am sure no other species would have remained in our presence before the advent of law and order. We would have killed all species thousands of years ago. We should have been fighting with ourselves right. Now we have started teaching manners to our pet animals, but what about people? Who is going to teach us? I am sure no prophet, no angel or alien is going to teach us. In fact we should learn these manners from our animals, for example, loyalty from a dog and the like. We are now behaving like wild animals… even animals may feel ashamed watching our activities. I will tell you a joke but there is a lesson. We should feel ashamed on our thinking, activities and our mindset.

Two or three dogs were at a square, a bitch came from somewhere and stopped by, scenting their presence. A dog suddenly said, "We are not humans, go. We are not going gang rape then kill you. Do you think a woman is in the place of that bitch? What will we do? We will assault her sexually, then we shall make sure she will die, to escape from law and order safely."

Many times, I have seen that if you try to harm a monkey, all the other members of the group will try to hurt you. They display such care and unity for their group members. We have started making groups on Whatsapp or Facebook, but in real life, we belong to no group nor we want to join or make any group for any body's welfare, we make groups only to destroy humanity and our nature. Another example is when you are going to feed the birds, especially crows, called an ecological niche in biology, but I have personally seen the crow start making noise to attract other crows' attention. When we look at what we humans are doing, we would even kill a person for a loaf of bread. I feel embarrassed to call myself a human being right now.

What we need is to change the programming of our mindset slightly so that we will also become compassionate, will show some kindness, honesty, love, affection and care for others. When are we going to leave our conservative mindset? When will we learn to love each other without thinking of its return? To love the opposite sex only for a particular reason is not love. Yes it is true, we should do that, but share your love with others too, some times with strangers who need it more. Share a loaf of bread with a hungry old man, it gives immense pleasure I swear. Now see the following examples, by which you can very well guess the general mind set of most people.

Look the pathetic condition of our selfish minds: a story of my best friend and what has happened to him just for a thousand rupee note, he was almost killed in the capital of India, i.e. Delhi. My friend went on a leisure tour. He boarded a flight from Srinagar to Delhi. From the Delhi airport he was picked up by a radio taxi which dropped him at New Delhi railway station. He enquired about the train schedules for Agra. He was very new to the city as somebody came to know by the way he was making enquiries. So someone took advantage of this weakness. A well-dressed person came to him and told my friend that he too is going to Agra. There were no seats available for that day and the best option was to travel by bus as it was hardly a four hour journey from Delhi to Agra. My friend is a very straight-forward person, kindhearted and has a bad habit of trusting people blindly. Within no time he starts believing strangers. This habit put him in big trouble. On his way to ISBT Kashmiri gate from New Delhi railway station, he and the other stranger took a rickshaw. The stranger offered him some water and biscuits. Those food items were altered and some toxicants were added as he was not aware; after eating them, he fell unconscious. He was carrying some clothes in a bag, a mobile phone, a watch and one thousand rupees in his wallet, two ATM cards and some essential documents and all of them were looted and he was beaten in his unconscious condition and was thrown in a gutter.

Next day he was found by police, naked and in bad condition and was admitted in a nearby hospital. After two days he was able to make a call to his brother to describe his sad story. He was so badly ill that for two days he could not remember his home phone number also. This is Delhi for you at present, look how people are treated, and what is the value of human life? Just one thousand rupees, not more than that. Even animals have more value today as compared to human beings. This is humanity at our best in the 21st century. We can take any step to go for any type of crime. Where is the humanity? Instead of guiding him in a new city, he was almost killed. What was his fault? Only that he trusted that person, was this his crime? What it depicts is that we should not trust anyone in this world, trusting people means harming ourselves. That means we are only to earn money here. what about if we are called honest, trustworthy, helpful, kind hearted? Isn't that enough for a common man? Look, money can buy you a costly bed not a peaceful sleep, luxuries but not culture, medicines but not health, religion but not salvation, food but not appetite and at last a passport to everywhere but not heaven.

Now I want you to read this beautiful poem, "**once upon a time**" by **Gabriel Okara**. My all-time favorite poem, and I am memorizing it daily. It is in fact a meaningful poem. This poem depicts the true face of people in modern times. The poet wishes that the modern world would once become innocent and childlike. He also wishes that he could once again be as natural, honest, and innocent as when he was a child. I suggest you read this poem and understand what the poet wants to convey. First I will give the summary of this beautiful poem.

Summary

The poet tells his son about the behavior of people in the past and in the present, in the olden days and in the modern world. He remembers a time when people had true feelings for one another. They would laugh from the heart and meet one another with genuine feeling. But today in the modern, busy world people often greet each other without any warmth in their handshake. They greet each other with a smile or a laugh that does not reach their eyes or warm their hearts. When they say 'come again' to a guest they don't really mean it, they only say it to be polite. According to the poet, people these days are often interested in meeting people only if they are rich, powerful, successful or famous, and do not value or respect those who have no wealth or position.

Have you ever said something nice to someone without meaning it? Why do you think you said it? Was it because you were too busy and did not think about what you were saying? Was it because it was the correct thing to say in that situation? To be a part of the society we need to learn behavior that is accepted in society. We begin to learn this as we grow up and behave according to the situation we are in. We learn this behavior so well that our natural behavior slowly disappears, and in each different situation we behave in the way that is considered appropriate for that situation. The poet says that he behaves very differently in the office, compared to the way he behaves at a party, or on the street. And none of these different faces that he puts on is his natural self or his real face.

He says that he has also learned to say things that he doesn't really mean, because they are the correct things to say in that situation. For example, when we are introduced to someone we are taught to say, "Glad to meet you." So the poet says that he too sometimes politely greets a person in this way even though he may not be interested in meeting him or her. The poet feels sad that like other adults in today's world he has forgotten how to be a natural person.

The poet has a deep desire to go back to the innocence of childhood. He is dissatisfied with his own changed self. He thinks that his son's genuine laughter can teach him how to express his feelings honestly. He wants to relearn how to behave in a natural way. He wants to get rid of the falseness in his behavior that makes his laugh unpleasant, because he laughs with his lips and teeth and not with his eyes and heart.

Poem

Laugh
but mean it

Do not fake it

ONCE UPON A TIME

Once upon a time, son,
they used to laugh with their hearts
and laugh with their eyes:
but now they only laugh with their teeth,
while their ice-block-cold eyes
search behind my shadow.

There was a time indeed
they used to shake hands with their hearts:
but that's gone, son.
Now they shake hands without hearts: while
their left hands search
my empty pockets.

'Feel at home!' 'Come again':
they say, and when I come
again and feel
at home, once, twice,
there will be no thrice –
for then I find doors shut on me.

So I have learned many things, son.
I have learned to wear many faces
like dresses - homeface,
officeface, streetface, hostface,
cocktailface, with all their conforming smiles
like a fixed portrait smile.

And I have learned too
to laugh with only my teeth
and shake hands without my heart.
I have also learned to say, 'Goodbye',
when I mean 'Good-riddance';
to say 'Glad to meet you',
without being glad; and to say 'It's been
nice talking to you', after being bored

But believe me, son.
I want to be what I used to be
when I was like you. I want
to unlearn all these muting things.
Most of all, I want to relearn
how to laugh, for my laugh in the mirror
shows only my teeth like a snake's bare fangs!

So show me, son,
how to laugh; show me how
I used to laugh and smile once
upon a time when I was like you.

-Gabriel Okara

Who is poor? A wealthy women goes to a saree store and tells the salesman, "Show me some cheap sarees. It is my son's marriage and I have to gift it to my maid." After some time, the maid came to the saree shop and tells the same salesman, "Show me some expensive sarees. I want to gift it to my mistress on her son's marriage." Poverty is in the mind or in the purse?

Who is rich? Once, a lady with her family was staying in a star category hotel. She was a mother of a four month old baby. "Can I get a cup of milk ?" asked the lady to the manager. "Yes madam", he replied. "But it will cost you a hundred bucks." "No problem", said the lady. While driving back from the hotel, the child was hungry again. They stopped at a road-side tea vendor. "How much?" she asked the vendor. "Madam, we do not charge money for a child's milk", the old man said with a smile." Let me know if you need more for the journey." The lady took one more cup and left. She wondered, "Who's richer? The hotel manager or the tea vendor?"

Sometimes, in the race of money, we forget that we are all humans. Let us help someone in need, without expecting something in return. It will make us feel better than money.

Coffee never knew that it would taste so nice and sweet, before it met sugar and milk. We are good as individuals but become better when we meet and blend with the right people. Stay connected - the world is full of nice people. If you can't find one, at least become one.

What I observe about the feelings in my heart when I was in Chennai, we were four people staying in our hostel room i.e. myself, one from Shimla and two south Indians. During my whole tenure there, I remain stuck to Rajesh who was from Shimla. We used to study together, eat together, play together, conduct city tours together. We were fast friends there. The other two were not enemies but what both of us thought was we are North Indians so we should stay together, it was a different feeling which was generated in our minds.

After our graduation from there, we moved to New Delhi for higher studies, where most of the students were from north India, that north India feeling vanished from our minds. We were feeling relaxed. In Delhi, we met new people. For a while, Rajesh and I remained together until we met the students of our own state. Now the feeling of being North Indians had shifted to our state feeling. In Delhi, I met Ravi who was from Jammu and at the same time my north Indian friend Rajesh also met people from Shimla. After that, we changed our rooms with consent. We both got separated day by day after our studies were over. Ravi and I applied for jobs in Jammu, both got selected and moved to our own state. For some time we showed the same care for each other; then we met other employees of our division. Now the feeling of "state-hood" was over, a new feeling was generated, that was of "division-hood" meaning the Jammu division and the Kashmir division.

Now assess the condition in all cases. People were the same, only the situation changed, which directly changed our feelings. We can generate it at any time in any situation for anybody, so why not all the time? Can't we change our feelings for human beings so that we can live friendly and peacefully without any wars and aggression?

So what is wrong with us? Where has the love, affection, honesty, tolerance gone now? Who is going to teach us why we are doing this? Let's take some time to think it over. I am going to place a few examples in the following chapters to make you aware of where we are wrong and what steps are to be taken for remedial action. Maybe in the future we shall save our humanity and our nature, so that we will put in some effort to conserve our earth for our generations to come. We will make it worth living not only for ourselves but also for every creature which is living here.

What will happen if you take a injured man to hospital? Your time and effort can save somebody's life. Maybe it will be you on some other day; you also may need someone's hands to save you. Your life is as precious as another's.

Women

Show the world that you are raised by a queen and loved by a princess.

The role of a woman, by taking into analysis the biological, psychological, and social dimensions, is of maximum importance for development of children first and then the whole society. The basic traditional role is to nurture and educate children, discipline them, manage the home and support the family. To raise your children properly, you are also required to teach and educate them, to prepare their child to face the real world and the basic learning of walking, talking, reading and writing as we all know. Another main thing is to provide the children with the best education and to establish and maintain order in the family by setting a certain level of discipline.

Why do girls get married and go to a new house? It is because they are blessed angels of the Almighty, after filling their own home with color of happiness, they go away to color others' homes, so we must realize their value and respect them. We need women as a mother, as a sister, as a wife, even as a girlfriend, but not as a daughter. Men get ultimate love and affection from their mothers, then from sisters, then the role of the wife, then after that it is your daughter. If we understand that a women is so caring and affectionate, nobody can replace her in this role. If we can view the role of any mother of any living being, the mother loves her child more than her own life and she will do anything for their betterment. I am not going to write down all the roles that a mother has to play; a man gets his women in the form of a mother, sister, wife, and daughter, and man is incomplete without women. He is raised, cared, loved by women thought his life. A common mentality of our Indian society is that all domestic work should be taken care of by women - if a man does housework, he feels inferiority or shame which is totally wrong. A woman is not supposed to work 24x7 without any leave or break. They have their own wishes and likes that they sacrifice for their home and family, but in turn what do they get instead of a reward or a compliment? We all know how we treat them; their condition is so pathetic and miserable. We try our level best to keep them suppressed, emotionally and physically.

In India women are not safe - they cannot even travel alone, can't go outside during night, cannot work with dignity and cannot even get her basic rights! She has been tortured starting from her pre-birth to post birth lasting her whole life. Women cannot even enjoy their basic freedom and liberties. They need to be handled with love, affection and care. Before stepping outside their homes they have to think several times if it is safe and if they are properly dressed. She cannot wear the dress of her choice! She is forced to wear what society demands of her! Choice does not exists anywhere!

Today, if we pick up any newspaper on any day, what we find is news about brutal rapes, human trafficking and forced prostitution, domestic violence, dowry killing, marital rapes, mistreatment of widows, female foeticide, forced abortion, forced pregnancy and so on. Even in the twenty first century, they are not safely enjoying their rights and not living life as per their choice, they are being tortured by men. They sacrifice everything as a mother, as a wife, as a daughter, as a sister. Let me tell you a story that happened recently. We were in our office, and a colleague of mine picks up the newspaper and starts laughing after reading some portion of that newspaper. I told him to please share the joke with us so that we can also refresh our minds. What he saidshocked us all. There was a news article about a gangrape which had happened a few days ago. His actual words were, "Oh she was raped by three men, how much she had enjoyed!" This was what he was laughing about. This is the present mentality of our educated folks, what can we expect from the uneducated lot? They are supposed to learn from educated people but most of the crimes are done by educated white collar professionals.

Now close your eyes for some time and think: are women only considered as sex objects? The semantic meaning of crime against women is direct or indirect physical or mental torture to women. The most effective plans are likely to be those that support women by organizing peer groups and mobilizing community resources and women's services. Such approaches enable women to overcome resignation to their legitimacy, to their established order or important factor in their perpetuation of imbalance of power between women and men. If women have to implement their reproductive preferences that the implementation occurs within their personnel spheres and that of community.

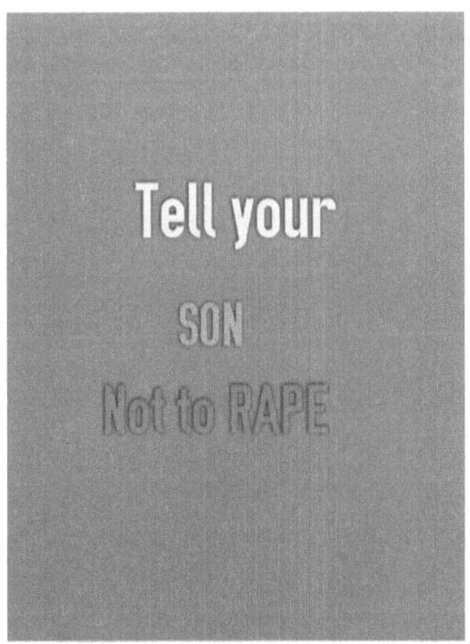

How can anybody rape? To ruin some body's life for a mere ten minutes of pleasure? Where are the social values and morality? They are not even afraid of law and order or to face social shame. If somebody does the same to our sisters, what would we do? I am sure we will go to any extent to counter it. We want our sisters to be saints and for the rest of the women to be horny for us. Now I will shed some light on the problems which women are facing today and their remedial actions. Women have been facing violence for a long time, specifically rape and sexual assault. These incidents often go unreported or under–reported. It is widely recognized that even today lack of reliable data is a hindrance in having a clear picture of violence against women. It can occur in public and private parts of life and at any time of their life. Below is the table which shows violence against women throughout their life cycle.

PHASE	TYPE OF VIOLENCE
Pre-Birth	Sex selective abortions
Infancy	Female infanticide
Girl Hood	Child marriage Female genital mutilation physical sexual and psychological abuse child prostitution
Adolescence	Physical sexual and psychological abuse partner violence martial rape dowry forced pregnancy forced prostitution
Elderly	Physical and psychological abuse

Now I will shed some light on the crimes against women, so that we can know how many problems they face in our society and how to overcome them. It is not an easy task but a tough one. Until and unless our mentality changes, nothing can happen. Day by day, the crimes against them will increase and the world will become hell for them to live in.

1. Female foeticide
2. Child marriage
3. Domestic violence
4. Exploitation at work place
5. Abduction, Rape and Murder
6. Defamation
7. Forced pregnancy
8. Adultery
9. Marital Rape
10. Owner Killing
11. War Rape and sexual slavery during military conflict
12. Female genital mutilation
13. Breast ironing

Here we need not define these headings. All of us are well aware what is happening around us. Every day, our society faces this shame but we just ignore it by saying "this is none of our business or our concerns" until we are victims, then only we will come to know actual pain caused by the above heading. I will now place some small stories which happen on a day to day basis but we ignore them as usual. Being a good citizen not only of our country but of the whole world, we have to be concerned about every ill aspect of our society, and we should join hands to eradicate this menace until and unless we don't see others in pain. Nobody has time or concern for these crimes. This should be a national issue and we should perform it like a duty. Only then we will save our society. All our social and moral values remain intact. Following are some stories which will give us some idea of what is happening around us so that all of us can be vigilant and conscious.

(A) Haridawar, 2015: To this day, I don't know why I agreed to go to his house. He was my yoga teacher, in his early thirties. One night he asked me to stay behind after class. "Why don't you come to my house tonight?" I refused politely, saying we might have guests at home and I had to go home early.

But he wouldn't take no for an answer, and eventually I ran out of excuses. At his house, he offered me tea and we went to the kitchen. I tried to stay on topic but he kissed me and pulled my clothes off, swearing he wouldn't tell anyone. I begged him to stop, but he raped me and then lay next to me. I felt so sickened, but I couldn't do anything. He raped me multiple times over three months, saying he loved me and wished to marry me. Everyone knew how upset I was, but I couln't bring myself to tell them what was happening to me. It ended only when I moved away from that city with my family. Today I realize he took advantage of a naïve teenager and abused his position of trust. No one should be allowed to do that.

(B) New Delhi, 2014: A five year old girl died after being raped in the capital city of India. A five year old girl was kidnapped, raped by two men who then abandoned her in the living room. The girl suffered cardiac arrest and died at a hospital while she was being treated. India has seen a recent sharp rise in the number of rapes and sexual crimes against women and children.

(C) Ranchi: An eighteen-year-old girl was raped and set on fire on the terrace of her home. The teenager was found her parents who heard her screaming from the terrace. She was then taken to hospital and remain in critical condition with serious burns over most of her body. She was raped, beaten and set on fire by a man who had been stalking her.

(D) Miraj: A story of a woman who was raped by her husband. Rape itself is a disturbing word to listen, and marriage is a most auspicious thing. But when these two elements combine, the result is horrible as we all can guess. Not all marriages are safe, some are horrifying nightmares as well. This is story of a victim who was raped by her husband. He forced her into sex against her wish and then continued to do it until she couldn't bear it any longer. Her husband raped her daily. He forced himself on her, every single day, even on the days she bled. He didn't stop all through the pregnancy. Marriage is not a certificate to rape. People failed to understand that a wife is not a machine to enjoy sex, bear kids and take care of the family. She is an individual, with her identity and has equal rights to live her life the way she wants.

(E) New Delhi: Who can forget the national shame that occurred on 16th December 2012? Nirbhaya, a twenty three year old medical student was raped, beaten and tortured by six men on a Delhi bus. She was violated with an iron rod during the assault and thrown from the moving bus, dying two weeks later. The brutality of the attack prompted fierce criticism of the police, rows in Parliament and protested in which tens of thousands of people on the streets. The government responded by rushing through legislation to double the presents terms of rape, and by criminalizing voyeurism, stalking and trafficking of women.

(F) Jhunghunu District (Rajasthan): A man was arrested for raping his eighteen-year-old daughter; the girl was abused for more than four years by her father, asked a friend to film her rape to collect evidence and convince her mother, who refused to believe the harrowing tale. the girl recorded a video the act and produce it as an evidence as evidence in front of the police and registered an FIR. Her father has been sexually abusing her for last four years whenever she told her mother, she refuse to believe her, she shot a video with the help of her friend to prove her point. She wants her father to be punished.

(G) Kerala: we have seen the case of a law student who was raped and murdered in cold blood. She lived in a single room with her mother. She was found by her mother when she came from work. She had severe head injuries and wounds were found on her chest and face. Her private parts were slashed and her intestines and abdominal organs were pulled out. To ensure her death her rapists smothered her.

(H) Maharashtra: In an extremely shocking and disgusting incident, a newly wed girl is called "not virgin" by Nasik's village caste panchayat after they were informed of her failing 'virginity test' by her husband. What is more disgraceful is that the man is permitted to end his marriage with the girl whom he wed hardly forty eight hours ago. Just one day post marriage, man was provided a white bed sheet by the panchayat which instructed him to return it shortly after his first night. When he didn't find any blood stains on the bed sheet and showed the same to the panchayat, it permitted him for terminating his wedding.

(I) There are many other ways through which hymen may break and it is not always necessary that it breaks while making physical relationship with a guy. In fact lots of physical exercise also result in the same and if a girl doesn't bleed in the first night, it is not necessarily that she isn't virgin. What is more, whether a girl is virgin or not is determined by blood on the first night but what are the measures of determining whether a man is virgin or not? Now see the condition in 21st century in commercial capital of India. Our panchayat will decide which girl is suitable and which is not. See the standard of our mentality, isn't it the time to change it otherwise it will be too late.

If you wear saree, you will get raped
If you wear jeans, you will get raped
If you wear veil, you will get raped
So, the problem is not the dress
If you are seven, you will get raped
If you are seventeen, you will get raped
If you are seventy, you will get raped
So, the problem is not age
If you are Hindu, you will get raped
If you are Muslim, you will get raped
If you are Christian, you will get raped
So, the problem is not her religion
If you are a mother, you will get raped
If you are a daughter, you will get raped
So, the problem doesn't lie in her societal status
Then, where is the problem?
The real problem is within us. No law and order can change us, unless we change ourselves so why to blame the system, change the culture
Believe in humanity
Be a man, respect women.

Now we can see openly that age, relation, and situation is no bar in sexual violence. Women are being tortured everyday. It is extremely disgusting and disgraceful that the whole nation is infected with this disease. They are not safe anywhere, not even in their home. There are many ways by which we can counter this horrible menace which has taken control of our society. Following are the challenges faced by a women in assessing justice. Examples:

- lack of criminalization,
- lack awareness of their existing laws,
- challenges in making a case in court.

Proper education is needed at the base level to change this mentality:

- Strict laws to be implemented.
- Moral education to be given at all levels.
- Women police stations to be opened.
- Fast track courts to be made for sexual crimes so that victims gets justice on time.

There is one single surefire way of ensuring that women don't get raped – and it is by teaching men not to do it. When we hear about these rapes, our heads hang in shame. In every home, parents ask daughters lots of questions as to where she is going, when will she return, and ask her to inform them when she reaches her destination. But have we ever asked your son where is he going and who are his friends? After all, the person committing the rape is also someone's son.

Lack of suitable and law enforcement machinery has added to the problem. During the time of kings, the punishment for the crime was hard and harsh and there was no delay in giving justice. But today the bigwigs are involved in rapes because they know the law cannot go against them. So need of the hour is to make laws tougher to tackle such persons.

Elders

Read this beautiful story, you will come to know where our minds have reached.

A son took his father to a restaurant to enjoy a delicious dinner. His father was of advanced age, and obviously weak too. While he was eating, a little bit of food fell from time to time on his shirt and table. The other diners watched the older man with their faces distorted in disgust, but his son remained totally calm. Once both were done eating, the son, without being remotely ashamed, helped his father by taking him to the washroom. He cleaned up the leftovers from his wrinkled face, and tried to wash the stains of food from his clothes. He lovingly combed his hair and finally got his glasses cleaned. On the way out, a profound silence reigned in the restaurant. The son was going to pay the bill and got ready to escort his father out of the restaurant. Just then a man rose from his chair among the diners, and asked the son, "Don't you think that you have left something here?" The young man replied, "No, I haven't missed anything here." Then the stranger said to him "Yes, you've left something. You left here a lesson for each child and for each parent." The entire restaurant was so quiet, you could hear a pin drop.

From the story the key take away is that we have forgotten the duty of taking care of our elders. As we saw, all the diners looked in shock, as if he was an alien, doing all that to his father. We forget he was also among us. If we would have been doing the same, what he was doing, then every diner should have ignored the scene. But it was out of way, I can say that is why all looked so shocked. Why can't every son be like that? Some people will feel ashamed while doing that in our society these days. We forget our parents have done the same, even more than we can think of. Returning the love and care that we took from them, that should be our priority.

One of the greatest honors that exists, is the privilege of taking care of our elders who cared for us. Our parents, and all the elderly family members who sacrificed their lives, giving us their time, money, effort and unconditional love.

They deserve our utmost respect and care. Read this beautiful story, you will come to know where our mind has reached. We forget our foremost duty and responsibility towards our parents. And those who fulfill theirs are very few days. We have become so materialistic and selfish that we forget our own parents.

A son and his old mother were in their room. His mother was very old and frail. A bird came and sat on the window, as there was some noise created by that creature. The old lady asked her son, "What bird is that?" The son said, "It is a pigeon, mom." After a few minutes mother asked again," What bird was that?" The son again replied, "It was a pigeon." After a few minutes the mother asked the same question again, and this time the son got angry and yelled, "Shut your mouth, I told you three times it was a pigeon." For a few minutes the mother remained silent then she told her son, "When you were a child, the same thing happened to me. A pigeon sat on the same window and you asked me twenty times which bird that was. I replied twenty times without getting angry like you just did." The son felt ashamed. We forget what our parents do starting from our conception to our entire childhood.

I will tell you another story. A ninety four year old woman, old and weak, was taking care of her disabled sixty three year old son. They lived together in a wooden house. Her son was unable to walk from birth. His mother had taken care of him all his life. That is purely unconditional love that he recieved, just as we do from our parents. Now close your eyes and think: can you name one person who will do just ten percent of this to his mother. I am sure I will get a negative answer. When we grow up, we start ignoring our parents, their advice, their decisions. We take so much from them, and when they are useless to us we send them to old age homes instead of caring for them ourselves. How selfish we have become!

Another story I will tell you is about an old age home. A son put his parents in an old age home and went abroad. After a few years, he came back to see whether his parents were still alive. Thankfully they were. He told his father, "I hope you were fine here." The father replied, "Yes, my son. We enjoyed our stay here, but I want to tell you some problems that I faced. The fan is not working and there was no provision for a shower, so it was difficult to bathe." The son said, "Why are you complaining now after so many years? The father said that he had managed somehow, and didn't want his son to suffer when his children threw him in the same old age home. It is a simple equation: what we sow, we will reap. Your children will follow your examples, not your advice.

So this is the need of hour; to change our mindset regarding the welfare of our elders. Deep mentation is required in this regard. Elder abuse is very common, as we simply forget what our elders did for us throughout our whole life. What we do in return is shameful. Where has our moral values gone? How selfish and materialistic we became that we neglect our own parents. How shameful the act is, can u imagine? Elder abuse may be of many types like:

- Neglect: the refusal or failure to fulfill a care giving obligations, loss of respect for elders and lack of interest in the older person's well being
- Physical abuse: the infliction of pain or injury, physical coercion, or physical or drug –induced restraint
- Psychological abuse: it is also called as emotional abuse – the infliction of mental anguish. Discrimination on the basis of age, insults and hurtful words, false accusations, psychological pain and distress
- Sexual abuse: non- consensual sexual contact of any kind with the older person
- Financial or material abuse: the illegal or improper exploitation or use of resources of the older person. Theft of property, and extortion and control of pension money

Elder abuse dates back to earlier times initially seen as a social welfare issue and subsequently a problem of ageing, abuse of the elderly has developed into a public health and criminal justice concern these two fields ie. Public health and criminal justice have therefore dictated to a large extent how abuse of the elderly is viewed, how it is analyzed and how it is dealt with. The abused of the older people by the family members or others known to them, either in their home or in other residential areas. Concern over the mistreatment of the older people has been heightened by the realization that in the coming decades, in both developed and developing countries, there will be a sharp increase in the population in the older age segment.

Elder abuse is either an act of commission or of omission and that it may be either intentional or unintentional. The abuse may be of a physical nature, psychological nature or it may involve financial or other material maltreatment. Regardless of the type of abuse, it will certainly result in unnecessary suffering injury or violation of human rights. Whether the behavior is termed abusive, neglectful or exploitative will probably depend on how frequently the mistreatment occurs, it is duration, severity and consequences and above all, the cultural contest. For older people the consequences of abuse can be serious. Older people are physically weaker and more vulnerable than younger. Even a minor injury can cause serious and permanent damage. Many older people survive on limited incomes, so that the loss of even small sum of money can have a big impact. They may be isolated, lonely or troubled by illness.

The impact that physically and psychological violence have on the health of an older person is exacerbated by the ageing process and diseases of old age. It is more difficult for the elderly to leave an abusive relationship or to make correct decisions because of the physical and cognitive impairments that usually come with old age. In some places, kinship obligations and the use of the extended family network to resolve difficulties may also lessen the ability of older people, particularly women, to escape from dangerous situations. Often, the abuser may be the abused person's only source of companionship. Because of these and other considerations, preventing elder abuse presents a whole host of problems for practitioners. In most cases, the greatest dilemma is how to balance the older person's right to self-determination with the need to take action to end the abuse.

Efforts to galvanize social action against elder abuse at a national level and to develop legislation and other policy initiatives are at varying stages of development around the world. Despite a growing interest in the problem, most countries have not introduced specific legislation in elder abuse. Particular aspects of abuse are usually covered either by criminal law, or by laws dealing with civil rights, property rights, family violence or mental health. Specific and comprehensive legislation on the abuse of older people would imply a much stronger commitment to eradicating the problem. However, even where such laws exist, cases of elder abuse have only rarely been prosecuted. This is principally because older people are usually reluctant – or unable – to press charges against family members, because older people are often regarded as being unreliable witnesses, or because of the inherently hidden nature of elder abuse. As long as elder abuse is viewed solely as a caregiver issue, legal action is not likely to an effective measure.

Education and public awareness campaigns have been vital for informing people in industrialized countries about elder abuse. Education involves not only teaching new information but also changing attitudes and behavior, and is thus a fundamental preventive strategy. It can be conducted in a wide variety of ways – for instance, in training sessions, seminars, continuing educational programs, workshops, and scientific meeting and conferences. Those targeted will include not only practitioners in the various relevant disciplines – from medicine mental health and nursing to social work, criminal justice and religion – but also researchers, educators, policy – makers and decision – makers. A typical basic syllabus suitable for most disciplines includes an introduction to the topic of elder abuse, consideration of the signs and symptoms of abuse, and details of local organizations that can provide assistance. More specialized training courses will concentrate on developing skills in interviewing, assessment of abuse cases, and planning care programs. Even more advanced teaching from specialists in the field is needed to cover ethical and legal matters. Courses in how to work with other professionals and in multidisciplinary teams have also become part of advanced training curricula on elder abuse.

Public education and awareness raising are equally important elements in preventing abuse and neglect. As in public education on child abuse and intimate partner violence, the aim is to inform the general public about the various types of abuse, how to identify the signs and where help can be obtained. People who come into frequent contact with the elderly are a particular target for such education. Apart from family members and friends, they include postal workers, bank tellers, and electricity and gas meter readers. Educational programs aimed at older people themselves are usually more successful if the information on abuse is woven into wider topics such as successful ageing or health care.

The human rights of older people must be guaranteed worldwide. To this end:

- Existing laws on domestic or intra family violence should be extended to include older people as a group.
- Relevant existing criminal and civil laws should explicitly cover the abuse, neglect and exploitation of older people.

- Governments should introduce new laws specifically to protect older people.
- The problem of elder abuse cannot be properly solved if the essential needs of older people – for food, shelter, security and access to health care – are not met. The nations of the world must create an environment in which ageing is accepted as a natural part of the life cycle, where anti-ageing attitudes are discouraged, where older people are given the right to live in dignity – free of abuse and exploitation – and are given opportunities to participate fully in educational, cultural, spiritual and economic activities.

White Collar Corruption

In simple terms we can describe white collar corruption as a kind of corruption done by a high profile person in the course of his occupation. White collar crimes are non-violent, but criminals have a sense of entitlement and need for control. They are highly paid. This crime is on rise and is in fact increasing day by day. These criminals are very sharp minded, usually hard to catch. They remain hidden and their crimes are done silently without any violence. This is like a cancer in our society. Most of the people don't feel its presence, but are being cheated regularly in various forms. The earliest documented case of this kind of crime dates back to 15th century in England. An agent was caught stealing wool, which was supposed to be transported. Therefore the star chamber and exchequer chamber of English court of law adopted the "breaking bulk" doctrine as it constituted the crime of larceny. But nowadays they range from fake recruitment racketeers, ATM fraudsters, travel agents, property dealers, agents promising fake court affidavits. Apart from these, the legal profession, medical, education, engineering, corporate are involved at higher rate.

Medical: the medical practitioners are often involved in issuance of false certificates, carrying out illegal abortions, selling out sample drugs, even in some cases adulterated drugs and medicines to the patient'. Dilatory tactics are often adopted by them in providing treatment to their patients with a menswear to extract huge amount of money. Misleading and fake advertisement claiming absolute cure is also a frequent malpractices being carried out in this profession they simply commit crimes which are truly anti-social and creates damage to public health and safety at large. Actually people don't want to make compromise on their health issues that is why they people took that advantage and thus looting of general masses is carried out. They made people fools easily and then simply took large amount of money from them. Unnecessary tests and medical examinations are carried out to drain money from their pockets. One another issue is dragging of patients from government hospitals to private clinics n nursing homes in promising of better treatment. This practice is very common nowadays in India. Governments doctors have opened their own private clinics and nursing homes, they lure patients towards them directly or indirectly. They also force their patients to particular testing labs n checking "centers, from" where they get commissions for every test or examination. Now I will tell u a story which happened with me.

LEGAL

It is the most unfortunate thing at the same time devastating, because here the crimes are committed by these individuals who are given the responsibility to ensure law and justice. They forget the pious oath of serving the society and started looking for the legal loopholes. They made extensive study to try out ways for maximum tax evasion for rich corporates. Apart from tax evasion, there are very instances of unethical practices like that of fabricating false evidences, engaging professional witnesses, there by violating ethical standards of legal profession. They issue fake and false court affidavits to earn extra money.

ENGINEERING

We have seen many examples of losing human lives every day caused by the collapse or fell down of building or bridge or fly over or path holes on public roads. This is all because of this white collar engineering corruption.

We often find instances of underhand dealing with contractors, suppliers, passing of substandard works and maintenance of bogus reports of the labor works. They financially earn more for low grade works from the contractors, than they can earn for their genuine work. Therefore many of them, out of the greed of earning more and more play dangerously with thousands of lives of the individuals

EDUCATION

After medical, education is most affected by these white collar criminals. People don't want to make compromise on education of their children, they want best teaching faculty for their children. By this the professionals make use of it and took advantage of it. Teachers drag the students for taking private tuitions and even go to the extent of blackmailing them of ruining of their future, if they deny doing so. A nastier role is played by the private institutions that are least bothering in providing the education. Here also the government school teachers drag students to their coaching centers run by them during early morning or evening.They earn a lot of money from them. I have personally faced this problem during my school days. We were told that your syllabus is not going to complete here. You need some months of private classes. So the same staff of our school had opened a coaching center. As usual nobody wants to make compromise on studies, as we all were forced to take coaching. This is the condition of our education system. What to expect from other systems then?

SOCIETY:

The major white collar crime very common among the individuals, no matter he/she belongs to the middle or upper strata of the society is that of evading taxes. The complexity of the taxation laws provided a number of loopholes through which many individuals tried to escape. A tax evasion has known no professional or class boundary in our country. Be it an engineer, doctor, advocate, a business tycoon or a simple small industry trader-all have learned the trick of evading taxes. The main difficulty posed before the Income Tax Department is to acquire true information of the real and exact income of these professional. It is often alleged that only an insignificant amount of their total income is posed an income before the Income Tax Department and the rest therefore goes into the circulation as black money. The frequent modifications in the tax-laws of the country has been able to add very little to put a check on this continuing menace which is throwing a great negative impact in the Government revenue and thereby the growth of the country.

CORRUPTION AT HIGHER LEVEL:

"Corruption threatens the integrity of markets, undermines fair competition, distorts resource allocation, destroys public trust and undermines the rule of law. Corruption is an old age phenomenon. The word corruption means destruction, ruining or spoiling a society or nation. Selfishness and greed are at the root of it. It also implies lack of integrity and honesty. a corrupt society is characterized by immorality and lack of fear or respect for the law. It has many forms ranging from bribery, misappropriations of public goods, nepotism and influencing the formulation of laws or regulations for private gain.

According to the Oxford dictionary, corruption means – "perversion of destruction of integrity in discharge of public duties by bribery or favor".

According to the world bank, corruption is defined as "abuse of public power for private benefit".

Corruption is widespread in India. India has been ranked out of 176 countries in transparency international's 2012 corruption perception index (CPI). Corruption has taken role of a pervasive aspect of Indian politics and bureaucracy. Now have a look of its extension in our society at present times:

- **Real estate**: It was said apartments with a valve of USD1.8 million were sold for USD130000 each in the apartment block. Three of the Maharashtra CM Ashok chavan's relatives were involved
- **Sports**: Match fixing, Commonwealth games scam, IPL fraud, nepotism in IPL
- **Health**: Jharkhand medical equipment scam of worth Rs 130 crores, and many other scams
- **Telecom:** A Raja was recently sacked after a CAG report said his ministry sold 2G licenses below market rates costing India nearly $40 billion dollars
- **Software**: the founder of Satyam, one of the top service firms in India admitted he had falsely inflated profits for years and resigned in Jan 2009
- **Judiciary**: In Jan 02 S.P.Bharucha, then the Indian chief justice said 20% of the higher judiciary might be corrupt. As of Feb 2006, 33635 cases were pending in the supreme court and more than 3 million cases were pending in high courts
- **Defense**: army ration pilferage scam, jeep scam in 1948, helicopter deal

In recent years so many major scams involving high level public officials have shaken the Indian public services. These scams suggests corruption has become a pervasive aspect of Indian political and bureaucratic system some of the major scams are:

- 1992 – harshad Mehta scam was worth rs 5000 crores
- 1994 – sugar import scam was worth rs 650 crores
- 1995 – preferential allotment scam was worth 5000 crores
- 1996 – Bihar fodder scam was worth 950 crores
- 1997 – Bihar land scam was worth rs 1200 crores
- 1998 – teak plantation scam was worth 8000 crores
- 2001 – ketan parekh security scam was worth rs 1250 crores
- 2002 – sanjay Agarwal home trade scam was worth rs 600 crores
- 2003 – telgi stamp paper scam was worth rs 172 crore
- 2005 – scorpene submarine scam was wort 18978 crores
- 2006 – Taj Corridor Scam was worth 175 Crores
- 2008 – Pune Billionaire Hasan Ali tax default scam was worth Rs 50,000 crores
- 2008 – Satyam Scam, was worth Rs 10,000 Crores
- 2008 – Army Ration Pilferage Scam was worth Rs 60,000 Crores
- 2008 – 2G spectrum Scam was worth Rs 60,000 Crores
- 2008 – State Bank of Saurastra Scam was worth Rs 95 Crores
- 2008 – Illegal money in Swiss Bank I worth Rs 71,00,000 Crores
- 2009 – Jharkhand Medical equipment scam was worth Rs 130 Crores
- 2009 – Rice export scam was worth Rs 2500 crores
- 2009 – Orissa Mine scam was worth Rs 7000 crores
- 2009 – Madhu Koda scam was worth Rs 4000 crores
- 2010 – IPL fraud involving swine called Lalit Modi option yet to be fixed

- 2010 – Commonwealth Games scam, Quantum of loot yet to be fixed
- 2010 – Reddy brother's illegal mining activity, recently arrested by CBI on High Courts directive, Quantum of loot yet to be fixed

Corruption is a global phenomenon and it is omnipotent. It has progressively increased and is now rampant in our society. Corruption in India has wings, not wheels. As the nation grows, the corrupt also grew to invent new methods of cheating the government and public. The cause of corruption are many and complex. The following are some other causes of corruption:-

- Emergence of a political elite which believes in interest oriented rather than nation oriented programmers and policies.
- Artificial scarcity created by people with malevolent intention wrecks the fabrics of the economy.
- Corruption is caused as well as increased because of the change in the value system and ethical qualities of men who administer. The old ideals of morality, services and honesty are regarded as anachronistic.
- Tolerance of people towards corruption, complete lack of intense public outcry against corruption and the absence of a strong public forum to oppose corruption allow corruption to reign our people.
- Vast size of population coupled with widespread illiteracy and the poor economic infrastructure lead to endemic corruption in public life.
- In a highly inflationary economy, low salaries of government officials compel them to resort to corruption. Graduates from Indian institutes of management with no experience draw a far handsome salary than what government secretaries draw.
- Complex laws and procedures deter common people from seeking help from the government.

- Elution time is a time when corruption is at its peak. Big industrialists fund politicians to meet high cost of election and ultimately to seek personal favors. Bribery to politicians buys influences and bribery by politicians buys votes. In order to get elected, politicians bribe poor, illiterate people.

There are many myths about corruption which have to be destroyed if we really want to combat it :-

Public awareness is must to combat corruption in India, for this it should be must to improve our education system because education is the best mean to understand fundamental rights and Right – Wrong conversation.

Corruption can be remed if people can understand and start to believe the value of ethics and morality in their life. People will start to believe that their life is accountable if they really start to believe in God, in oneness of God and if they really start to live life on the way which God has chosen for mankind.

Foolproof laws should be made so that there is no room for discretion for politicians and bureaucrats. The role of the politician should be minimized. Application of the evolved policies should be left in the hands of an independent commission or authority in each area of public interest. The decision of the commission or authority should be challenged only in the courts.

Cooperation of the people has to be obtained for successfully containing corruption. People should have a right to recall the elected representatives if they see them becoming indifferent to the electorate.

Funding of elections is at the core of political corruption. Electoral reforms are crucial in this regard. Several reforms like state funding of election expenses for candidates, strict enforcement of statutory requirements like holding in party elections making political parties.

More and more courts should be opened for speedy and inexpensive justice so that cases don't linger in courts for years and justice is delivered on time.

Local bodies, independents of the government like Lok pals, Lok adalats and vigilance commissions should be formed to provide speedily justice with law expenses. The Strongest Lok Pal is must to remed corruption in India.

With the help of the Right to Information Acts, citizens should be empowered to ask for information related to public services, etc. and this information should be made available to general public as and when required. Such stringent actions against officials will certainly have a deterrent impact.

Therefore, the motto should always be prevention is better than cure. Since the acts involved defrauding public faith and belief, public as a whole mass should come forward to protect the whole society from these greedy people who are destroying the ethics and morality of the society slowly and slowly for their sole aim of pursuing narrow self.

It's a civil society initiative to push the government for comprehensive reforms of anti-corruption systems in India. Led by eminent people like Kiran Bedi & Anna Hazare and supported by various Right to Information activists, religious leaders and social reformers. Its created a voted bank against corruption http://www.voteforindia.org/ Indian citizens can register on this website and pledge that they will not vote for a party that doesn't support Jan LokPal bill.

JAN LOK PAL BILL

This anti-corruption bill was crafted by the IAC initiative as a response to governments watered down version of Lok Pal bill. Jan Lok Pal Bill is designed to create and effective anti-corruption and grievance redressed systems at center and to assure that effective deterrent is created against corruption and to provide effective protection to whistleblower. Lok Pal bill was first proposed in 1969 but could not get through Rajya Sabha. It has been introduced nine times since and failed each time. Anna Harare will be going on an indefinite fast from April5 2011 to convince Government to enact Jan Lokpal bill in place of PM'S watered down Lokpal bill. Jan Lokpal bill has a lot of support from various political parties- Sudhakar Reddy, AB Bardhan, Abani Roy (Left front), HD Devegowda (JDS) Mysore Reddy (TDP) and Jayant Choudhry (RLD) signed a joint statement indicating their support to the movement.

CORRUPTION'S TIME HAS COME LETS STAND AGAINST IT TOGETHER

Dowry

An officer who has cleared UPSC exam by writing a good essay on dowry and its effects on social and financial life of people demands dowry more than the uneducated class. There are various forms of dowry ranging from cash, jewelry, cars, property. If a girl is born, they will kill the girl because they can't bear the expenditure of dowry.

My neighbor who is a security personnel sold his property to cover the dowry payment. He has one daughter who completed an MBA in finance. But when the time of her marriage came, she was not getting a suitable match as the price of such matches was so high that his father was not able to pay. She was then ready to make compromise for unsuitable match for her. Even she was ready to get married with an intermediate pass boy. But her father was having great expectations, he wouldn't allow her to do the same. Now look how much her father have spent on her throughout her life starting from her birth even before her birth. How many sacrifices he has made for her daughter to make her future glorious and smooth! But what does our society gave him and her daughter in reply? Just a simple message that girls don't need higher education, if they will get and you are not able to pay dowry all of your sacrifice and handwork will go in vain. Finally he was forced to sell his property to pay the dowry to a boy who was less educated than her daughter and was earning less than her. In spite of lesser education and lesser salary she was forced to pay dowry. Why not the boy will pay to her father as he made her capable of everything , he sacrifices all his wishes for her daughter Her father was helpless. This is our society, here depicts how much educated we are, how much cultured we are. What was his fault only he make her daughter to get higher education, to pursue her dreams but what he got was all her dreams were ruined by dowry in a single stroke?

Another story I will tell you of a bold girl who fights for her rights:

In our India where most young girls succumb silently to their fate, seldom taking their own decisions. The story of a young girl on the threshold of marriage, who informs the police about her bridegroom's illegal demands on her family and gets arrested. A twenty five year old Anjali did the remarkable job. Just as she was about to be married, Anjali filed a police complaint against her groom for demanding excessive dowry. Anjali's bold and gutsy actions have turned her into a national heroine overnight. Anjali an engineer by profession, filed a complaint in a police station in a city in Jammu, after her husband-to-be, Rakesh Malgotra, roughed up her father at the wedding, while demanding an additional ten lakhs in dowry. But her father had already given a huge amount worth roughly the same.

Mr. Rakesh Malgotra was demanding more from her father. Anjali took the bold decision and the culprits were arrested with in no time. Anjali decision undoubtedly followed her father's firm stand; her father told that if he marries her, their long lasting demands wouldn't end and they will start blackmailing on every phase.

The practice of asking for dowry from a bride's parents was officially outlawed by the Indian government in 1961, but is still widely followed. According to police sources, only 2–3% of women dare to report dowry harassment to the police. Most of them are people from urban areas. Laws should be made firm and culprits should be given punishment, in fact severe punishments. Everyone should support this to eradicate this disease from our society. Anjali's bold decision changed the minds of so many victims. Having become an icon for other girls, Anjali has one piece of message that never yield to dowry demands and do not afraid to stand up for your rights people who harass dowry should be taught a lesson.

Here I will paste a letter of a father, whose daughter was murdered only after forty five days of her marriage by her husband and in-laws for not accepting their dowry demands.

To all Indian girls who are going to get married and their parents.

From December on wards is the marriage season in India, and perhaps you are planning your wedding. I also got my beloved daughter married on 12 Dec 2009, with the man of her choice. A man she was in love with and wanted to marry. I got her married so happily with all pomp and shows as happens in all educated middle class families in India. But what has been the outcome of that marriage? We lost our beloved daughter – as it feels that we lost everything in our life. It is too painful for me to even describe the whole episode here.

But my main aim is to write this is to spread a message to the brides who will get married this wedding season and to the families'. Please, please be cautious before saying YES to any groom and his family. Please beware that even you think the husband loves you, like my daughter thought her husband did, the husband can change from the very next day after the marriage and no longer what you expect him to be. And not only that, but the husband and his family once start demanding more dowry, their greed does not stop. It only gets bigger and bigger and they want more and more after the bride goes to their house.

As a father of three daughters please accept my practical life experience –and I say this to all young Indian women who will be nice brides, and to their family.

I don't want any girl and her family to go through this life like us. The pain and agonies of a grieved family are beyond the imagination and description on all fronts. The joys of life vanishes forever. Even today after two years, the family of her is not able to attend any marriage. In every bride girl they see the face of our beloved daughter and it becomes very painful and beyond control to stay in those moments of happiness. So to avoid the family of friends and brides, we have decided not to attend any marriage till the gods give us strength to do so.

We know the pain and agonies of losing our daughter, who was just like any ordinary girl, full of passion, of ambition, extremely beautiful and fair, having everything in her life. She was very bold and ambitious girl and was working in a US based multi-national company and getting handsome salary. She loved us so much that she could not bear that we may go up to such despair over the game that destiny played with her life. She left all family weeping. The happiness and joy of our family has vanished away forever it seems. In the absence of our beloved daughter, our ultimate aim is that no girl or family in India and world should face such tragic sufferings

In the legal sense, dowry means any property or valuable security given or agreed to be given, either directly or indirectly, by one party to a marriage to the other party at or before or after the marriage as a consideration for the marriage of the said parties.

Dowry is a custom turned as a social evil. The concept of equality among martial relationship is toppled by the custom. Moreover human dignity of women is questioning through the custom. Women who don't have enough money are the most sufferers. Most of them is denied martial life or right to choose appropriate spouse. Justice is denied to the females and the custom is beneficial to male. There is ample evidence that the phenomena of dowry is expanding to communities where it had never existed, and that the value of dowries is rising to untenable limits. There are horrific reports of fathers selling their property to cover dowry payments and even sometimes selling their organs .

Dowry is any item or cash given by the bride family to the grooms' family at the time of marriage. Dowry is a major problem with Indian marriages; dowry related violence can occur when the dowry or bride-price is seems to be insufficient to the grooms family. Dowry id bride-price that gives the position of daughter-in-law to any girl in someone's family. It can be added that dowry is a social custom and it is very difficult to change customs all of a sudden; practicing customs generate and strengthen solidarity and cohesiveness among people; many people give and take dowry only because their parents and forefathers had been practicing it.

In spite of the fact that practice of dowry became illegal in 1961 and it is still flourishing among all social classes. The youth can definitely play a key role in eradicating this evil practice the cases of dowry free marriage. Till the time, younger generation musters courage to stop this practice and girls resist social pressure to take it, people will stick to this custom.

In the present scenario dowry system as it is practiced in India, it has become an instrument of torture for the bride and her parents and family. Majority of women reporting domestic violence gave dowry demands as the primary cause of violence against them and also they have faced all kinds of violence i.e. physical, psychological/emotional and verbal. The results of the present study are in line with these findings. People of all economic status and educational background have demanded dowry and indulged in domestic violence when this demand has not been fulfilled. In this study also people of all economic background demand dowry and indulged in domestic violence however majority of cases were reported from lower and middle class families (55% and 33%) which is quite alarming. Women experiencing marital violence were more likely to have been depressed, and to have had low self-esteem.

In the study it was revealed that one out of every four dowry victims was driven to suicide due to extreme mental and physical torture. The torture begins when the in-laws harass the women for more gifts, cash jewelry, household items and appliances from her family this problem becomes severe when girl child born in the family as out of forty cases reported here 85% females had girl child. Forty cases of dowry related domestic violence were studied here from western UP, India Majority of women in the present study experiencing dowry related domestic violence got married in their early age 52.5%, from rural background (55%). Present study suggests a link between domestic violence and dowry demands, it also indicates that there are some contributory factors for this like lower household income, lower educational background, having girl child, type of marriage (Love/Arranged/Love-cum-arranged) and type of family (nuclear, joint, extended). The result of this study indicates that economic empowerment, together with higher education and modified cultural norms may protect the women from such type of social evil.

I request all my countrymen to take a pledge against the dowry system. We can eradicate this disease in our society. Let us launch an open war against it. Take a pledge that you will not accept dowry in any form: cash, property or gifts even if offered and at the same time you will not give dowry that is demanded of you.

Caste System

How strange it is that Dalit women are being raped very day, forced to prostitution, but are denied the right to use the services of public utilities like wells, public transport, as well as education institutes. No one practices untouchability when it comes to sex. Rape is a common phenomenon in rural areas. Women are raped as a part of caste custom. Moreover, if you pick up any newspaper you will find out yourself how much they are harassed by upper classes, paraded naked several times. Don't they have their own self-respect, dignity? Women are sold into flesh trade. This leads to the greater incidence of child marriage especially in rural areas. Dalit women are also raped as a form of retaliation. They are raped as a part of an effort by upper-caste leaders to suppress movement to demand payment of wages, to settle sharecropping disputes, or to reclaim lost land. Dalit women face the triple burden of caste, class and gender.

The untouchables are given a very low position in the society. Upper-caste people will allow dogs in their homes but will not tolerate any untouchable entering their home. Strange but true. Just think for a while they are humans too. When will we change our mentality? We are in the 21st century, but still living in the medieval times by our thinking. Why do we maintain a social distance from them? They are denied many basic amenities of life. They are denied to enter the religious institutes. The untouchables were neither allowed to enter the temples nor served by the Brahmans. They had no right to worship the Gods and Goddesses in the temple.

The untouchables are not free to choose any occupation according to their ability. Now look how much talent might have got wasted. Some people are talented by birth, but if we did not allow them to pursue their career as per their talent, then we are simply wasting their talent and losing innovation and progress. Mostly they were landless laborers. They worked in the fields of the upper-caste people. They suffered from many economic problems. They had to face many financial hardships and they were not given wages for their service. They were not allowed to carry out any business. Still in some rural areas, they are not permitted to engage themselves in professions which are engaged in by the people of other castes.

Traditionally they were deprived of getting education. Today you will find most of them are illiterate. They were not allowed to use public education institutes. Now reassess the situation: if our former president Dr. APJ Abdul Kalam had been among them,what would have been the result? We could have lost a real gem in India only because he was born in such a family that is only supposed to clean our streets, remove dead cattle and to undertake heavy agricultural work. Now think about how many talented people we have lost because of our cheap mentality. Earlier it was worse, but now it is reduced, but more education is required to eliminate this disease from our country. God has created humans in His image, He has not made any discrimination in His creation. Who are we to discriminate on the basis of just caste? This bloody word has ruined lives of millions of people without any reason or excuse. Just think, for God's sake, we all are one. No one is superior and no one is inferior. We should not discriminate on the basis of caste, creed sex, religion or color. It will give you immense pleasure if you pay respect to these people. This is one trait of the armed forces that I like, that they don't discriminate, and they practice excellent discipline; sleeping under the same roof, working towards the same goal.

Despite the fact that "untouchability" was abolished under India's constitution in 1950. The practice of "untouchability" – the imposition of social disabilities on person by reason of their birth in certain castes – remains a very much a part of rural India "untouchables" may not cross the line dividing their part of the village from that occupied by higher classes. They may not use the same well, visit the same religious institute, drink the same cups in tea stalls, or claim the land that is legally theirs. Their children are made to sit in the back of class room, and communities as a whole are made to perform degrading rituals in the name of caste.

People still follow this caste system even in adverse conditions. I have seen personally in a hospital a child was having some serious problem, I don't know what exactly he was suffering from. But what I know was he has to go under surgery and blood was needed. They were asked by the medical staff to collect blood from the blood bank. What his parents said will shock you and I too was shocked. After hearing their water I went outside, took a glass of water, sat on a bench outside and looked up to sky and asked God, "Why did you create such kind of people?" Their answer was, "No we will not take blood from a blood bank we don't know whose blood is that, we will call people from our own caste to collect blood." Now see the situation and their cheap mentality. On one side their child's life is at stake, and on the other side they are not going to change their mentality for a silly thing. Though they were good looking, well-educated but their mentality was so cheap even today in the 21st century. If a person doesn't change his mentality in such a serious condition, I bet they never will and nobody can educate them. I know they can be literate but not educated.

Even today in our modern India, the Dalits are still treated as untouchables in the eyes of elite class. Having undergone three thousand years of slavery and discrimination, the Dalits find it nearly impossible to get out of this terrible trauma. The general situation of these people is miserable. More and more Dalits continue to live in extreme poverty, without land or opportunities for better employment or education. With the exception of a minority who have benefited from India's policy of quotas in education, government jobs. Dalits are relegated to the most menial of tasks, as manual scavengers, removers of human wastes, and dead animals, leather works, street sweepers. Dalit children make up the majority of those sold into bondage to pay off debts to upper class creditors.

In India the caste system developed and is prevalent since ancient times and it remains as great thorn in the growth of Mother India. The origin is of caste system could be the functional grouping, Called Varna's, which have their origins in the Aryan society. "According to the Rig Veda hymn, the different classes sprang from the four limbs of the Creator. The Creator mouth became the Brahman priests, his toe arms formed the Rajanya (Kshatriyas),the warriors and kings, his two thighs formed the Vaishya, landowners and merchants and form his feet were born the Shudra (Untouchables) artisans and servants. Then it is believed that the caste system had been adopted by the Brahmins to express their superiority. When the Aryan races swept into India. They wanted to maintain the superiority and so they maintained the caste systems. Gradually the caste system became formalized into four major groups, each with its own rules and regulations and code of conduct.

Caste in Indian society refers to a social group where membership is largely decided by birth. This caste system became fixed and hereditary with the emergence of Hinduism and its beliefs of pollution and rebirth. The Laws of Manu (Manusmitri), refer to the impurity and servility of the outcastes, while affirming the dominance and total impunity of upper castes. Those from the "lowest" castes are told that their place in the caste hierarchy is due to their sins in their past life. Vivid punishment of torture and death are assigned for crimes such as gaining literacy or insulting a member of a dominant caste. Manusmitiri, the most authoritative text of Hindu religion legitimizes social exclusion and introduces absolute inequality ad the guiding principle of social relations.

Caste still very much matters to Indian citizens even in the modern world though one must point out that different groups of citizens have different reasons for maintaining the system of caste. The upper castes want to keep caste alive to oppress the lower castes thereby maintaining their dominating. It is very interesting to note that the lower caste groups, who are supposed to hate the caste system, also want to use their caste identity to gain benefits in the corridors of power and politics and, at the same time, they want to put a stop to the caste oppression imposed upon them by the upper castes. It is an ironical and interesting situation of the Indian society I modern India.

Actually, it was meant to show that the four classes stood in relation to the social organization in the same relations as the different organs of the Primordial Man to his body. Together they had to function to give vitality to the body politic. But the caste system grown to the level of retarding the growth of an individual in the same of caste and there by affecting the fundamental rights of an individual to live or to grow which is the Essene of democracy. How caste system affects the democracy can broadly be classified under two headings.

There were many movements and governments actions that took place pre-and post-independence in order to overcome and attempt to eliminate the inequalities and injustice associated with the caste system. During the national movement Gandhi began using the term "Harijans" (God's people) to refer to the untouchables in order to encourage a shift towards positive attitude towards the lower castes. Many lower caste members, however, found the terms to be patronizing. The Census of Indian had started by the British in the late 19th century, and in 1935 the British Government of India came up with a list of 400 groups considered untouchable, as well as many tribal groups, that would be accorded special privileges in order to overcome deprivations and discrimination. Those groups included on this list came to be termed Scheduled Casted and Scheduled Tribes. In the 1970s however, many leaders of castes considered untouchable started calling themselves Dalits. The anti-caste Dalit movements began with Jyotirao Phule in the mid-19th century, and he started a movement for education and the up liftmen of women, Shudra's and Dalit's, and the movements spread to many parts of Indian. He also worked to abolish the idea of untouchability, which meant getting rid of restrictions on entry into temples, and finding a place for Dalits within Hinduism.

Another prominent movement was the Dalit movement under B.R. Ambedkar, which began between the 1920s and 1930s.He campaigned for greater rights for Dalit's in British India, and even after independence. Ambedkar and Gandhi were advocates for the abolishment of the caste system, but they disagreed on the means to go about it. Gandhi believed untouchability to be a moral issue that could be abolished through goodwill and change of heart among the upper-caste Hindus. Ambedkar, however believed that he subordination of Dalits was primarily economic and political, and could only be overcome by changing the social structure through legal, political, and educational after independence that reserved a certain percentage of seats in elections for Dalits, but by the mid-1950s Ambedkar was not satisfied by the rate of implementation the measures. He encouraged around six million Dalits to convert to Buddhism as a means of escaping the social stigma of untouchability within the Hindu caste system. During the 1970s the Dalits panthers movement sprouted up among the younger generation of Dalits along with other social movements in India, and their movements expressed their anger and frustration at the failure of implementations regarding policies that would eliminate acts of violence against Dalits by upper – caste Hindus in many parts of urban and rural India.

The caste system cannot be eradicated without changing the mindset of the people. The system is a great social evil. From time to times social reformers and thinkers have tried to eradicate this evil but to no avail. It is a deep-rooted problem which has defied all solutions so far. The problem has persisted largely becomes of the illiteracy and ignorance of the people. Their ignorance makes the people conservative and superstitious. Hence they do not accept any social change. They want things to continue as they are. Every measure of social reform is strongly opposed and is considered to be an attack on their religion by the religious fanatics.

Therefore, if the evil of caste system is to be eradicated every possible effort should be made to educate the people and thus create a strong public opinion against the evil. School text books should be carefully revise. Lesson should be included to reach the students that the caste system is manmade. It was a system for the division of labor devised by our wise forefathers. Originally man was not born into any caste and his caste was determined by his learning or by the nature of work he did in life, basically, all human beings are equal; they have the same kind of blood in their veins. The different of upper and lower are wrong and the entirely the creation of vested interests. The similarities between the different the different castes should be stressed rather than the different castes should be stressed rather than the differences, in this away awareness would be created against the caste system and its hold upon society would be gradually loosened.

Communial Violence

CHAPTER I
PRELIMINARY

Short title, extent and commencement

1. (1) This Act may be called the Communal Violence (Prevention, Control and Rehabilitation of Victims) Act, 2005.

(2) It extends to the whole of India except the State of Jammu and Kashmir

(3) It shall come into force in the Union territories on such date as the Central Government may, by notification, appoint.

(4) The provisions of this Act except Chapters II to VI (both inclusive), shall come into force in the states on such date as the Central Government may, by notification in the Official Gazette, appoint and different dates may be appointed for different provisions of this Act and the provisions of Chapters II to VI(both inclusive), shall come into force in a State as the State Government, by notification, appoint and any reference to any provision of this Act to the commencement of this Act shall, in relation to a State, be construed as a reference to the commencement of that provision in that State.

Definitions

2. (1) In this Act, unless the context otherwise requires:

(a) "Code" means the Criminal Procedure Code, 1973;

(b) "communally disturbed area" means an area declared as such under sub-clause(i) of clause (c) of sub-section (I) of section 3 or under clause (a) of sub-section (3) of section 55;

(c) "communal violence" means any act of omission or commission which constitutes a scheduled offence and which is punishable under section 19; 2 OF 1974

(d) "competent authority" means such officer or authority as the State Government or the Central Government may, by notification, appoint as the competent authority under sub-section(4) of section 3 or as a Unified Command under sub-section(4) of section 55, as the case may be;

(e) "District Council" means the District Communal Disturbance Relief and Rehabilitation Council established by the State Government under sub-section(I) of section 42;

(f) "District Fund" means the Victims Assistance Fund established by the State Government under section 51;

(g) "National Council" means the national Communal Disturbance Relief and Rehabilitation Council constituted by the Central Government under sub-section(I) of section 45;

(h) "notification" means a notification published in the Official Gazette;

(i) "period of disturbance", in relation to a communally disturbed area, means the period during which it is to be a disturbed area for a purposes of section 3 or section 55, as the case may be;

(j) "prescribed" means prescribed by rules made under this Act;

(k) "relief and rehabilitation" includes providing shelter, medical care, food, clothing, education, vocational training and counseling or such other measures of relief as may be considered necessary by the State Council or the District Council to the victim of communal violence;

(l) "scheduled offence" means an offence specified in the schedule;

(m) "Special Court" means a Special Court constituted under sub-section(J), or an additional Special Court established under sub-section(2), of section 24;

(n) "State Council" means the Communal Disturbance Relief and Rehabilitation Council established by the State Government under section 39;

(o) "State Fund" means the state Communal Disturbance Relief and Rehabilitation Fund established by the State Government under sub-section(l) of section 49;

(p)"Unified Command" means the authority constituted by the Central Government or the State Government under sub-section(4) of section 55.

2. The words and expressions used and not defined in this
Act but defined in the Explosives Act, 1884 or the Arms
4 of 1884. Act,1959 shall have the meanings respectively assigned to
54 of 1959. them in those Acts.

CHAPTER II
DECLARATION OF CERTAIN AREAS AS COMMUNALLY DISTURBED AREAS

3.(1) Whenever the State Government or the Central Government is of the opinion that one or more scheduled offences are being committed in any area by any person or group of persons-

(a) in such manner and on such a scale which involves the use of criminal force or violence against any group, caste or community resulting in death or destruction of property; and

(b) such use of criminal force or violence is committed with a view to create disharmony or feelings of enmity hatred or ill will between different group, caste or communities; and

(c) unless immediate steps are taken there will be danger to the secular fabric, integrity or internal security of India;

Power of State Government to declare certain areas as communally disturbed areas

it may by notification,-

(i) declare such area as communally disturbed area; and

(ii) constitute such area into a single judicial zone or into as manu judicial zones as it may deem fit.

(2) A notification under sub-section (1) in respect of any area shall specify the period during which the area shall, for the purpose of this Act, be a communally disturbed area;

Provided that the period specified in such notification shall not, in the first instance, exceed thirty days, but the State Government or the Central Government as the case may be, may amend such notification to extend such period from time to time by any period not exceeding thirty days at any one time, if in the opinion of that Government public peace and tranquility continues to be disturbed in such area.

(3) Where any area has been notified as a communally disturbed area under sub-section (1), then, it shall be lawful for the State Government or the Central Government to take all measures, which may be necessary to deal with the situation in such an area.

(4) (1) Where a State Government has declared an area to be a communally disturbed area under sub-section(l) of section 3, it shall take such immediate measures as may be necessary to prevent and control communal violence in such area.

(2) If the State Government is of opinion that assistance of the Central Government is required for controlling the communal violence, it may request the Central Government to deploy armed forces of the Union to control the communal violence.

Measures to be taken by State Government on declaring a communally disturbed area.

CHAPTER III
PREVENTION OF ACTS LEADING TO COMMUNAL VIOLENCE

Power of District Magistrate to take preventive measures etc.

1.(1) Notwithstanding anything contained in the Code, whenever the District Magistrate has reason to believe that in any area within his jurisdiction, a situation has arisen where there is an apprehension of breach of peace or creation of discord between members of different groups, castes or communities, he may, by order in writing, prohibit any act which in his opinion is likely to cause apprehension in the minds of another community or caste or group that it is directed to intimidate, threaten or otherwise promote ill will against that community or caste or group.

(2) Notwithstanding anything contained in sections 6,7,9 and 10 the District Magistrate shall also have the same powers as the competent authority has in the area under his jurisdiction in relation to the provisions of the said sections.

(3) Whoever contravenes an order under this section shall be punished with imprisonment for a term, which may extend to one year, or with fine, or with both.

Power of competent authority to take preventive measures

6. (1) A competent authority in any area within his jurisdiction which has been notified as a communally disturbed area, by order in writing:-

(i) direct the conduct of any assembly or procession in any place or street and specify by general or special notice the routes, if any, by which and the times at which, such procession may or may not pass;

(ii) require, by general or special notice, on being satisfied that any person or class of persons intend to convene or collect a assembly or a procession in any place or street or to form an assembly or procession which would in his judgment, if uncontrolled, is likely to cause a breach of peace that the person convening or collecting such assembly or procession or directing or promoting such assembly or procession shall not do so without applying for and obtaining a license; and

(iii) prohibit or regulate the use of loudspeaker, music or sound amplifier or any other noisy instrument in any street or public place or in any private place if the use of which may cause annoyance to neighbors.

(2) A order under sub-section(i) shall remain in force for such

Power to order deposit of arms & ammunition etc	period as may be necessary or thirty days, whichever is less: Provided that the State Government, after reviewing the effect of the order, if considers it necessary for the preservation of communal peace or harmony between different groups, castes or communities or public safety or maintenance of public order in such area, may, by notification, direct that the order issued under sub-section(l) shall remain in force for such further period not exceeding sixty days from the date of the first order.	
Power to search, detain and seize arms etc. in communally disturbed areas	7.(1) When any area has been notified as a communally disturbed area, then notwithstanding anything contained in any law for the time being in force, competent authority may direct, any person or class of persons, or all persons, in a communally disturbed area, to deposit forthwith all arms, ammunition, explosives and corrosive substance, with the nearest police station, whether such person has a license to keep such arms, ammunition, explosives, corrosive substance, or not; Provided that a competent authority may exempt any individual or class of individuals from the operation of such order. (2) whoever contravenes the provisions of an order made under this section, shall be punished with imprisonment of either description, for a term which may extend to three years and shall also be liable to fine. 8.When ever any area has been notified as a communally disturbed area, then notwithstanding anything contained in any law for the time being in force, if any officer in charge of a police station has reason to believe- (a) any person residing in the limits of his jurisdiction within a communally disturbed area has in his possession any arms or ammunition, or explosives or corrosive substance, for any unlawful purpose: and (b) such person cannot be left in the possession of any arms or ammunition, or explosives or corrosive substance, without danger to the public peace and safety, the officer in charge of the police station may himself or any another officer, not below the rank of a Sub-Inspector of Police authorized in this behalf by the officer in charge, search the house or premise occupied by such person or in which the officer in charge has reason to believe that such arms or ammunition, or explosives or corrosive substance, are, or is to be, found, and may have such arms, or ammunition, or explosives or corrosive substance, if any, seized, and detain the same in safe custody for such period as he thinks necessary although the person may be entitled by virtue of any law for the time being in force to have the same in his possession.	

	9. (1) When any area has been declared communally disturbed area, then, notwithstanding anything contained in any law for the time being in force, any competent authority may in the areas under his jurisdiction, whenever and for such time as he may consider necessary, for the preservation of public, peace or public safety by a notification publicly promulgated or addressed to individuals, prohibits at any town, village or place or in the vicinity of any such town, village or place in a communally disturbed area- (a) the carrying of arms, cudgels, swords, spears, bludgeons, guns, knives, sticks or lathis, or any other article, which is capable of being used for causing physical violence; (b) the carrying of any corrosive substance or explosives; (c) the carrying, collection and preparation of stones or other missiles or instruments or means of casting or impelling missiles; (d) the exhibition of persons or corpses of figures or effigies thereof; (e) the public utterances of cries, singing of songs, playing of music; (f) delivery of harangues, the use of gestures or threats, and the preparation, exhibition or dissemination of pictures, symbols, placards or any other object or thing, which may in the opinion of such authority lead to a breach of public peace. (2) If any person goes armed with any such article or carries any corrosive substance or explosives or missile in contravention of such prohibition, he shall be liable to be disarmed or the corrosive substance or explosive or missile shall be liable to be seized from him by any police officer, and the article, corrosive substance, explosive or missile so seized shall be forfeited to the Government. (3) The competent authority may also, by order in writing, prohibit in a communally disturbed area any assembly or procession whenever and for so long as he may deem such prohibition to be necessary for the preservation of the public peace: Provided that no such prohibition ordered by an authority subordinate to the State Government shall remain in force for more than fifteen days without the sanction of the State Government. (4) The competent authority may, by public notice, in a communally disturbed area temporarily reserve, for any public purpose any street or public place and prohibit persons from entering the area so reserved, except under such conditions as may be specified by such authority. (5) Whoever disobeys an order lawfully made under this section, or	Power of competent authority to prohibit certain acts.

	abets the disobedience thereof , shall be punished with imprisonment for a term which may extend to three years and shall also be liable to fine.	
	10(1) Without prejudice to the provisions of any other law for the time being in force, a competent authority, in regard to a communally disturbed area, may make orders for- (a) controlling or regulating the admission of persons to, and the conduct of persons in, and in the vicinity of such area; (b) requiring the presence of any person or class of persons in such area, to be intimidated to any prescribed authority, specified in the said order; and (c) prohibiting any person or class of persons from being in possession or control of any article specified in the said order. (2) Whoever contravenes any order made under this section, without just and sufficient cause, shall be punished with imprisonment for a term which may extend to three years and shall also be liable to fine.	Power to make orders regarding conduct of persons in communally disturbed area
Punishment for loitering near prohibited places	11.(1)No person loitering in, or in the vicinity of, any communally disturbed area shall continue to loiter in, or in that vicinity after being ordered to leave it, by a police officer, or any other person authorized in this behalf by the competent authority. (2) Whoever contravenes the provisions of this section without just and sufficient cause shall be punished with imprisonment for a term which may extend to one year, or with fine, or with both.	
Punishment for being in possession of arms etc. without license.	12. Whoever, being present within a communally disturbed area, has in his possession any arms, ammunition, explosives or corrosive substance without any license or lawful authority, shall be punished with imprisonment for a term which may extend to three years and shall also be liable to fine.	
Punishment for assisting offenders	13. Any person who knowing or having reasonable cause to believe that any other person has committed any act or omitted to do an act, the commission or omission of which, would be an offence under the provision of this Act, gives that other person any assistance with intent thereby to prevent, hinder or otherwise interfere with his arrest, trial or punishment for the said offence, shall be punished with imprisonment for a team which may extend to three years and shall also be liable to fine.	
Punishment for giving Financial	14. Whoever knowingly expends or supplies any money in furtherance or in support of an act which is an offence under this	

aid for the commission of certain offence	Act, shall be punished with imprisonment for a term, which may extend to three years, and shall also be liable to fine.	
Punishment for threatening witnesses etc.	15. Whoever, threatens any person- (i) who is, or is likely to be, a witness in any prosecution for an offence under this Act, or in any trial before a Special Court constituted under this Act: (ii) Who has in his possession or knowledge any material document or other information which if produced before an investigating officer, or a court, could be used as evidence in the investigation for an offence under this Act, or in a trial before a Special Court constituted under this Act: (iii) With any injury to his person or property or to the person or property of any one in whom that person is interested, with intent to cause harm to that person, or to compel that person to refrain or withdraw from being a witness in such investigation or trial, or to prevent that person from producing such material, document or information before the investigating officer or court as mentioned aforesaid; Shall be punished with imprisonment for a term which may extend to three years and shall also be liable to fine.	
Driver, owner or any persons in charge of goods transport vehicle not to carry more persons than authorized.	16. Whoever being the owner, driver or otherwise in charge of goods transport vehicle carries or causes to be carried in a vehicle in a communally disturbed area, any number of persons in excess of the numbers permitted under the Motor Vehicles Act, 1988 or the rules made thereunder, shall be punished with imprisonment for a term which may extend to one year, or with fine, or with both.	59 of 1988
	17.(1) whoever being the public servant or any other person authorized to act by a competent authority under any provisions of this Act or orders made thereunder- (a) Exercises the lawful authority vested in him under this Act in a mala fide manner, which causes or likely to cause harm or injury to any person or property; or (b) Willfully omits to exercise lawful authority vested in him under this Act and thereby fails to prevent the commission of any communal violence, breach of public order or disruption in the maintenance of services and supplies essential to the community. Shall be punished with imprisonment which may extend to one year, or with fine, or with both. Explanation-------- For the purpose of this section, any police officer who, willfully refuses- (i) To protect or provide protection to any victim of communal violence;	Punishment for public servants acting in mala fide manner

(ii) To record any information under sub-section(l) of section 154 of the Code relating to the commission of any scheduled offence or any other offence under this Act,

(iii) To investigate or prosecute any scheduled offence or any other offence under this Act,

Shall be deemed to be guilty or willfully omitting to exercise the lawful authority vested in him.

(2) Not withstanding anything contained in the Code, no court shall take cognizance of an offence under this section except with the previous section of the State Government.

Provided that every request for the grant of sanction under this section shall be disposed of by the State Government within thirty days from the date of the request.

Punishment for violation of orders under section 144 of the Code in communally disturbed area

18. Not withstanding anything contained in any other law for the time being in force, whoever contravenes an order under section 144 of the Code, if that order is in respect of any person thing or any matter relating to a communally disturbed area under this Act, shall be punished with imprisonment for a term which may extend to three years and shall also be liable to fine.

CHAPTER IV
ENHANCED PUNISHMENT FOR COMMUNAL VIOLENCE

Punishment for committing communal violence

19.(1) whoever commits any act of commission or omission which constitutes a scheduled offence on such scale or in such manner which tends to create internal disturbance within any part of the State and threatens the secular fabric, unity, integrity or internal security of the nation is said to commit communal violence.

(2) Notwithstanding anything contained in the Indian Penal Code r in any other Act specified in the Schedule, whoever commits any act of commission or omission which constitutes communal violence shall, except in the case of an offence punishable with death or imprisonment for life, be punished with imprisonment for a term which may extend to twice the longest term of imprisonment and twice the highest fine provided for that offence in the India Penal Code or in any other Act specified in the Schedule, as the case may be:

Provided that whoever being the public servant or any other person authorized to act by a competent authority under any provision of this Act or orders made thereunder, commits communal violence shall without prejudice to the foregoing provisions be punished with imprisonment which shall not be less than five years.

45 of 1860

(3) Any person who is guilty of an offence under sub-section(l)

	shall be disqualified to hold any post or office under the Government for a period of six years from the date of such conviction.	
	CHAPTER V **INVESTIGATIONS**	
Scheduled offence to be cognizable	20.(1) notwithstanding anything contained in the Code or any other law, every scheduled offence shall be deemed to be a cognizable offence within the meaning of clause (c) of section 2 of the Code and "cognizable case" as defined in that clause shall be construed accordingly. (2) Notwithstanding anything contained in the Code, no police officer, below the rank of Sub-Inspector of Police or a police officer of equivalent rank shall investigate any offence punishable under this Act. (3) Section 167 of the Code shall apply in relation to a case involving a scheduled offence subject to the modification that the reference in sub-section(l) thereof to "Judicial Magistrate" shall be construed as a reference to "Judicial Magistrate or Executive Magistrate". (4) Section 366 to 377(both inclusive) and section 392 of the Code shall apply in relation to a case involving a scheduled offence, subject to the modification that the references to "Court of Session", wherever occurring therein, shall be construed as reference to "Special Court".	
Declaration of places to be police stations	21.(1) Whenever an area has been declared under sub-section(l) of section 3 as a communally disturbed area, the State Government shall, without prejudice to the provisions of clause(s) section 2 of the Code, declare any post or place within such area to be a police station and the provisions of Chapter XII of the code shall, so far as may be, apply in relation to information to the police and their powers to investigate. (2) The State Government shall provide as many women police officers as possible to record any information relating to the commission of a scheduled offence committed against women or children in the communally disturbed area and to investigate any such offence.	
Constitution of review committees	22.(1) Notwithstanding anything contained in any other law for the time being in force, where the State Government comes to the conclusion that the investigation of offences committed in any communally disturbed area, and where the investigating officer does not file & charge sheet within a period of three months from the date of registration of the First Information Report shall be	

Constitution of special investigation teams	reviewed by an committee headed by an officer of the level of an Inspector-General of police to be constituted by the State Government and such committee may pass orders for a fresh investigation by another officer not below the rank of Deputy Superintendent of police wherever it comes to the conclusion that, having regard to the nature of investigation already carried out, such investigation would be necessary. (2) The committee constituted under sub-section(1) may also review cases of such offences where the trial ends in acquittal and issue orders for filing appeal, wherever (3) The committee shall submit a report of its findings and action taken in each cases or cases to the Director General of Police. 23. Notwithstanding anything contained in any other law for the time being in force, where the State Government comes to the conclusion that the investigation of offences committed in any communally disturbed area were not carried out properly in a fair and impartial manner it may constitute one or more special investigation Teams as it thinks necessary for the purposes of Investigation of such offences. **CHAPTER VI** **SPECIAL COURTS** 24.(1) The State Government may establish one or more special courts for trial of scheduled offences committed during the period of disturbance by issuing a notification for the purpose. (2) Notwithstanding anything contained in sub-section (1), if, having regard to the exigencies of the situation prevailing in a State, Additional special courts outside he State, for the trial of such scheduled offences committed in a communally disturbed area, the trial whereof within the State- (a) is not likely to be fair or impartial or completed with utmost dispatch; or (b) is not likely to be feasible without occasioning a breach of peace and grave risk to the safety of the accused, the witnesses, the Public Prosecutor and the Judge or any of them; or (c) is not otherwise in the interests of justice, it may request the Central Government to establish, in relation to such communally disturbed area, an Additional Special Court outside the state and thereupon the Central Government may, after	Establishment of special courts

	taking into account the information furnished by the State Government and making such inquiry, if any as it may deem fit, establish, by notification, such Additional Special Court at such place outside the State as may be specified in the notification. 25.(1) A Special Court shall be presided over by a Judge to be appointed by the appropriate Government with the concurrence of the Chief Justice of the High Court. (2) The State Government may also appoint with the concurrence of the Chief Justice of the High Court, Additional Judges to exercise jurisdiction in Special Court. (3) A person shall not be qualified for appointment as a Judge or an Additional Judge of a Special Court unless he is immediately before such appointment a Sessions, Judge or an Additional Sessions Judge in any State. (4) For the removal of doubts, it is hereby provided that the attainment by a person, appointed as a judge or an Additional judge of a Special Court, of age of superannuation under the rules applicable to him in the Service to which be belongs, shall not affect his continuance as such Judge or Additional Judge. (5) Where any Additional Judge or Additional Judges is, or are, appointed in a Special Court, the Judge of the Special Court may, from time to time, by general or special order, in writing, provide for the distribution of business of the Special Court among himself and the Additional Judge or Additional Judges and also for the disposal of urgent business in the event of his absence or the absence of any Additional Judge. 26. A Special Court may, if it considers it expedient or desirable so to do sit for any or its proceedings at any place, other than the ordinary place of its sitting, in the State in which it is established: Provide that if the Public Prosecutor certifies to the Special Court that it is in his opinion necessary for the protection of the accused or any witness or otherwise expedient in the interest of justice that the whole or any part of the trial should be held at some place other than the ordinary place of its sitting, the Special Court may, unless, for reasons to be recorded in writing, the Special Court think fit to make any other order. 27.(1) Notwithstanding anything contained in the Code or in any other law, a scheduled offence, committed in a judicial zone in a	Composition and appointment of Judges of Special courts Place of sitting Jurisdiction of special courts

	State at any time during the period during which such judicial zone is, or is part of a communally disturbed area shall be triable, whether during or after the expiry of such period, only by the Special Court established for such judicial zone in the State: Provide that where the period specified under sub-section (2) of section 3 as the period during which an area declared by notification under sub-section (1) of that section to be communally disturbed area commences from a date earlier than the date on which such notification is issued, then- (a) nothing in the foregoing provisions of this sub-section shall apply to a scheduled offence committed in such area in which the whole of the evidence for the prosecution has been taken before the date of issue of such notification; and (b) all other cases involving scheduled offences committed in such area and pending before any court immediately before the date of issue of such notification shall stand transferred to the Special Court having jurisdiction under this section and the Special Court to which such proceedings stand transferred shall proceed with such cases from the stage at which they were pending at that time. (2) Notwithstanding anything contained in sub-section (1) If in respect of a case involving a scheduled offence committed in nay judicial zone in a State, the Central Government having regard to the provisions of sub-section (2) of section 4 and the facts and circumstances of the case and all other relevant factors, is of the opinion that it is expedient that such offence should be tried by the Additional Special Court established in relation to such judicial zone outside the State, the Central Government may make a declaration to that effect. *Explanation*—Where an Additional Special Court is established in relation to two or more judicial zones, such Additional Special Court shall be deemed, for the purposes of this sub-section, to have been established in relation to each of such judicial zones. A declaration made under sub-section (2) shall not be called in question in any court. Where any declaration is made in respect of any offence committed in a judicial zone in a State, any prosecution in respect of such offence shall be instituted only in the Additional Special Court established in relation to such judicial zone outside the	Scheduled offences to be cognizable

Powers of special courts with respect to other offences	State, and if any prosecution in respect of such offence is pending immediately before such declaration in any other court the same shall and transferred to such Additional Special Court and such additional Special Court shall proceed with such case from the stage at which it was pending at that time.	
	28. (1) When trying any scheduled offence, a Special Court may also try any offence other than the scheduled offence with which the accused may, under the Code charged at the same trial if the offence is connected with the scheduled offence.	
	(2) If, in the course of any trial under this Act found that the accused person has committed any offence, the Special Court may, whether such offence is or is not a scheduled offence, convict such person of such offence and pass any sentence authorized by law for the punishment thereof.	
Public Prosecutor	29.(1) For every Special Court, the appropriate Government shall appoint a person to be the Public Prosecutor and may appoint one or more persons be the Additional Public Prosecutors:	
	Provided that the appropriate Government may also appoint for any case or class of cases a Special Public Prosecutor.	
	(2) A person shall be eligible to be appointed as a Public Prosecutor or an Additional Public Prosecutor or a Special Public prosecutor under this section only if he has been in practice as a Advocate for not less than seven years or has held any post, for a period of not less than seven years, under the Union or a State, requiring special knowledge of law.	
	(3) Every person appointed as a Public Prosecutor or an Additional Public Prosecutor or a Special Public Prosecutor under this section shall be deemed to be a Public Prosecutor within the meaning of clause (u) of section 2 of the Code, and the provisions of the Code shall have effect accordingly.	
	30. (1) A Special Court may take cognizance of any scheduled offence, without the accused being committed to it for trial, upon receiving a complaint of facts which constitute such offence or upon a police report of such facts.	
	(2) Notwithstanding anything contained in the Code, the Special Court shall conduct its proceedings on a day to day basis excluding public holidays.	
	(3) Where a scheduled offence is punishable with imprisonment for a term not exceeding three years or with fine or with both, a	
	Special Court may, notwithstanding anything contained in sub-section (1) of section 260 or section 262 of the Code, try the offence in a summary way in accordance with the procedure prescribed in the Code and the provisions of section 263 to 265 of the Code shall, so far as may be, apply to such trial.	

	Provided that when, in the course of a summary trial under this sub-section, it appears to the Special Court that the nature of the case is such that it is undesirable to try it in a summary way, the Special Court shall recall any witnesses who may have been examined and proceed to re-hear the case in the manner provided by the provisions of the Code for the trial of such offence and the said provisions shall apply to and in relation to a Special Court as they apply to and in relation to a Special Court as they apply to and in relation to a Magistrate: Provided further that in the case of any conviction in a summary trial under this section, it shall be lawful for a Special Court to pass a sentence of imprisonment for a term not exceeding two years.	
	(4) A Special Court may, with a view to obtaining the evidence of any person supposed to have been directly or indirectly concerned in, or privy to, an offence, tender a pardon to such person on condition of his making a full and true disclosure of the whole circumstances within his knowledge relative to the offence and to every other person concerned whether as principal or abettor in the commission thereof, and any pardon so tendered shall, for the purposes of section 308 of the Code, be deemed to have been tendered under section 307 thereof.	
	(5) Subject to the other provisions of this Act, a Special Court shall, for the purpose of trial of any offence, have all the powers of a Court of Session and shall try such offence as if it were a Court of Session so far as may be in accordance with such procedure prescribed in the Code for the trial before a Court of Session.	
	(6) Subject to the other provisions of this Act, every case before an Additional Special Court shall be dealt with as if such case had been transferred under section 406 of the Code to such Additional Special Court.	
	31. Whenever it is made to appear to the Supreme Court that an order under this section is expedient for the ends of justice, it may direct that any particular case he transferred from one Special Court to another Special Court.	Power of Supreme court to transfer cases
	32. (1) A Special Court may, on an application made by a witness in any proceedings before it or by the Public Prosecutor in relation to such witness or on its own motion, take such measures as it deems fit for keeping the identity and address of the witness secret.	Protection of witnesses

	(2) In particular and without prejudice to the generality of the provisions of sub-section (1), the measures which a Special Court may take under that Sub-Section may include- (a) the holding of the proceedings at a protected place; (b) the avoiding of the mention of the names and addresses of the witnesses in its orders or judgments or in nay records of the case accessible to public; (c) the issuing of any directions for securing that the identity and addresses of the witnesses are not disclosed.	
	(3) Any person who contravenes any direction issued under sub-section (2) shall be punishable with imprisonment for a term which may extend to one year and with fine which may extend to one thousand rupees.	
	33. Where after taking cognizance of any offence, a Special Court is of opinion that the offence is not a scheduled offence it shall, notwithstanding that it has no jurisdiction to try such offence, transfer the case for trial of such offence to any court having jurisdiction under the Court and the court to which the case is transferred may proceed with the trial of the offence as if it has taken cognizance of the offence.	
	34 (1) Where a Special Court is satisfied, upon a complaint or a police report that a person is likely to commit a scheduled offence in any communally disturbed area, it may, by order in writing, direct such person to remove himself beyond the limit of such area by such route and within such time as may be specified in the order, and not to return to that area from which he was directed to remove himself for such period, not exceeding six months, as may be specified in the order,	
	(2) The Special Court shall, along with the order under sub-section (1), communicate to the person directed that under sub-section the grounds on which such order has been made;	
Power to transfer cases to special courts	(3) The Special Court may revoke or modify the order made under sub-section (1), for the reasons to be recorded in writing, on the representation made by the person against whom such order has been made or by any other person on his behalf within thirty days from the date of the order.	
Removal of person likely to commit scheduled offence	35 (1) If a person to whom a direction has been issued under section 21 to remove himself from any area— (a) fails to remove himself as directed, or (b) having so remove himself enters such area within the period specified in the order, otherwise than with the permission in writing of the Special Court under sub-section (2), the Special Court may cause himself to be arrested and removed in police custody to such place outside such area as the Special Court may specify.	

Procedure on failure of person to himself remove area and from thereon enter removal after Appeal	(2) The Special Court may, by order in writing, permit any person in respect of whom an order under section 19 has been made, to return to be area from which he was directed to remove himself for such temporary period and subject to such conditions as may be specified in such order and may require him to execute a bond with or without surely for the due observation of the conditions imposed. (3) The Special Court may at any time revoke any such permission. (4) Any person who, with such permission, returns to the area from which he was directed to remove himself shall observe the conditions impose, and at the expiry of the temporary period for which he was permitted to return, or on the revocation of such permission before the expiry of such temporary period, shall remove himself outside such area and shall not return thereto within the unimpaired portion specified under section 19 without a fresh permission. (5) If a person fails to observe any of the conditions imposed or to remove himself accordingly or having so removed himself enters or returns to such area without fresh permission the Special Court may cause him to be arrested and removed in the police custody to such place outside such area as the Special Court may specify. 36(1) Notwithstanding anything contained in the Code, an appeal shall lie as a matter of right from any judgment, sentence or order, not being interlocutory, order, of a Special Court to the High Court both on facts and on law. (2) Except as aforesaid, no appeal or revision shall lie to any court from any judgment, sentence or order of a Special Court. (3) Every appeal under this section shall be preferred within a period of thirty days from the date of the judgment, sentence or order appealed from: Provided that the High Court may entertain an appeal after the expiry of the said period of thirty days if it is satisfied that the appellant has sufficient cause for not preferring the appeal within the period of thirty days.	Abolition of certain Special courts

37. Where any area ceases to be a communally disturbed area and no cases are pending before a Special Court or an Additional Special Court established in relation to such communally disturbed area, the State Government, may, by notification, abolish such Special Court or Additional Special Court, as the case may be.

State communal disturbance relief and rehabilitation council

Constitution of State Council

CHAPTER VII
INSTITUTIONAL ARRANGEMENTS FOR RELIEF AND REHABILITATION

38. Every State Government shall, by notification, establish a Council to be known as State Communal Disturbance Relief and Rehabilitation Council.

39. The State Council shall consist of the following members, namely:-

(a)the Chief Secretary of the State...ex officio Chairperson;

(b) the Director General of Police of the State...ex officio Member

(c) the Secretary of the Department entrusted with Relief and Rehabilitation work in the State Government-Members, ex officio;

(d) The Secretary of the Department of Finance in the State Government- Member-ex officio

(e) The Secretary of the Department of Home in the State Government-member, ex officio

(f)The Secretary to the Department of Social Welfare dealing with Tribal Welfare or minorities welfare or women and child Development in the State Government-member-ex officio

(g) Three persons to be nominated by the State Government to represent individuals or private voluntary organization engaged in the work relating to promotion of communal harmony or providing relief to the victims of communal violence-Members;

(h) not less than five persons to be nominated by the State Government in such a manner that all important religious groups in the State are represented in the State Council-Members;

(i) an officer not below the level of Joint secretary to the State Government to be nominated by the State Government-Member-Secretary, ex officio;

	j) the term of members appointed under clause(g) and (h) shall be such as may be prescribed by the State Government. 40 .(1) The Council Shall have the responsibility of planning relief and rehabilitation measures and co-ordination, monitoring and implementation of such measures and issue suitable directions for their implementation may be required. (2) Without prejudice to the generality of the provision of sub-section(1), the Council shall- (a) advise the State Government in matters relating to relief and rehabilitation of victims of communal violence including drawing up of guidelines for the assessment of compensation including grant of immediate or interim compensation which shall not be less than twenty percent of the full rates of compensation in respect of the losses suffered by an individual in communal violence in respect of-; i. loss of, or damage to, homes and belongings; ii. loss of life and injuries sustained; iii. destruction of, or damage to, business and the loss of means of livelihood; iv. impact of sexual assaults or abuse on women; (b) issue suitable guidelines for setting up of relief camps for victims of communal violence, which shall provide for the following:- i. arrangements for providing security at such camps; ii. appropriate shelter for winter, monsoon or summer seasons; iii. food, drinking water, toilet and bathing facilities; iv. health services, certification of injuries at the camp itself and issuance of medical cards with a validity of six months for purchase of free medicine, phychosocial support like trauma counseling; v. issue of temporary ration cards or other identity cards; (c) establish a system of single window to complete all administrative formalities in relation to providing quick relief and rehabilitation to the victims of communal violence including making available ration cards or other identity cards; (d) certify loss or damages of educational or other certificates or ownership or other documents in respect of the victims of communal violence; and facilitate the students of the area affected by communal violence to appear for any examination and to provide for the purpose;	Functions of Council

	(e) establish centers for rehabilitating the children of victims of communal violence; (f) establish a system of single window clearance scheme for speedy disposal of insurance claims and for providing soft loans by financial institutions or measures relating to rescheduling of loans and interest payments in cases of affected victims of communal violence in consultation with the financial institutions (g) facilitate the efforts of other organizations who may come forward to help the victims in all manner feasible. (h) recommend welfare measures to be adopted and implemented by the appropriate Government with a view to ameliorating the conditions of victims of communal violence; (i) draw suitable guidelines and issue directions for funding the restoration and repair of the places of worship damaged or destroyed during the communal violence, in consultation and with consensus of the members of the affected family; (j) formulate a comprehensive and affirmative scheme for welfare of victims of communal violence and devise a programme for implementing such schemes with the approval of the appropriate Government and implement the scheme; (k) activate the functioning of the district communal harmony committee; (l) maintain comprehensive data bank related to the social economic development of victims of communal violence; (m) report to the appropriate Government the inadequacies of shortcomings in any law for the time being in force and also on the remedial measures; and (n) perform such other functions as may be incidental or ancillary thereto as may be assigned by the appropriate Government from time to time. (3) While performing the functions under this section, the State Council shall follow such procedure as may be prescribed. 41.(1) The State Council shall prepare a plan for every state to be called the State communal harmony plan for promotion of communal harmony and prevention of communal violence, hereinafter called the State plan, and recommend the same to the State Government for adoption. (2) The State plan shall be prepared providing for- i. the measures to be adopted for prevention or mitigation of communal violence including the constitution of District	State plan for promotion of communal harmony and prevention of communal violence

	Level Peace Committees; ii. the capacity-building and preparedness of measures to be taken to deal with communal violence including a Riot prevention Scheme at the district and sub-district level. (3) The State Government shall adopt the State plan after such modification as considered necessary. (4) The State Government shall cause the Syaye Plan and also any advice, recommendation and guidelines issued under section 40 to be laid on the table of the State Legislature: Provided that where the State Government does not accept any of the recommendations of the State Council under section 40 or under this section, it shall apply expressly state the reasons for not accepting the recommendations and submit it along with the Action Taken report and cause the same to be laid on the table of the State Legislature as soon as may be while it is in session and where the State Legislation is not in session within fifteen days from the date of commencement of its session. (5) The State Plan shall be reviewed and updated every two years. (6) The State Government shall make appropriate provisions for financing the activities to be carried out under the State plan. 42.(1) The State Government shall, by notification, establish a District communal Disturbance Relief and Rehabilitation Council in respect of each district in the State. (2) The District Council shall consist of such number of members, not exceeding ten, as may be prescribed by the State Government, and unless the rules otherwise provides, it shall consist of the following members, namely:- (a) the Collector or District Magistrate or Deputy Commissioner, as the case may be, of the district who shall be the chairperson-Member, Ex officio (b) the Superintendent of Police of the District-Member, Ex officio (c) the Chief Medical Officer of the District-Member, Ex-Officio (d) such other district level officers of the Departments of Social Welfare, Tribal Welfare, Minority Welfare, Women and Child Development or such other Departments as may be prescribed by the State Government-Members-Ex-Officio; (e) two persons representing the private Voluntary organizations to be nominated by the State Government-Members; (f) not les than five persons to be nominated in such a manner that all important religious groups in the district are represented in the District Council-Members;	Constitution of District Council

	g) the terms and conditions of appointment of Members under clause(e) and (f) shall be such as may be prescribed by the State Government. 43. The District Council shall meet as and when necessary and at such time and place as the chairperson may think fit.	
Functions of District Council	44.(1) The District Council shall act as the district level coordinating and implementing body for relief and rehabilitation of victims of communal violence and take all measures for the purpose in accordance with the guidelines laid down by the National Council and the State Council including,- a. assessment of compensation in respect of losses suffered by an individual in communal violence in respect of- i. loss of, or damage to, homes, shops and such other structures and belongings; ii. loss of life and injuries sustained; iii. destruction of, or damage to, business and the loss of means of livelihood; iv. impact of sexual assaults or abuse on women; b. setting up of relief camps for victims of communal violence, including:- i. arrangements for providing security at such camps; ii. appropriate shelter for winter, monsoon or summer seasons; iii. food, drinking water, toilet and bathing facilities; iv. health services, certification of injuries at the camp itself and issuance of medical cards with a validity of six months for purchase of free medicine, phychosocial support like trauma counseling; v. temporary ration cards valid for specific period; (2) the District Council shall prepare a District Plan for promotion of Communal Harmony and Prevention of communal violence and recommend the same to the State Council. (3) The District Council shall periodically review the implementation of the orders passed by any Court for award of compensation to victims of communal violence under the provisions of this Act and submit an annual report to the State Council. **CHAPTER VIII** **NATIONAL COUNCIL** 45.(1) The Central Government shall, by notifications, constitute, with effect from such date as it may specify in such notification, a council to be known as the National Communal Disturbance Relief and Rehabilitation Council, consisting of not more than eleven members, to exercise the powers conferred on, and to perform the functions assigned to it by or under this Act.	
National		

<table>
<tr>
<td>Communal Disturbance Relief and Rehabilitation Council</td>
<td>(2) The National Council shall consist of following, namely-
i. the Secretary to the Government of India, Ministry of Home Affairs. member...ex officio;
ii. the Secretary to the Government of India, Ministry of Defense...ex officio Member
iii. the Secretary to the Government of India, Ministry of Finance-Members, ex officio;
iv. Four persons to be nominated by the Central Government representing Minority and weaker sections of the society; Member
v. Four persons nominated by the Central Government representing other sections of the society who have been striving to maintain the communal harmony-Members (3) The Central Government may appoint one of the members of the National Council as its Chairman.
46.(1) Every members of the National Council (other than the Ex official members) shall hold office for a term of four years from the date of their appointment.
(2) The traveling and other allowances payable to the members of National Council (other than the ex officio members) shall be such as may be prescribed by the Central Government.
47.(1) The national Council shall recommend to the appropriate Government as to-
(a) How the victims of the communal violence should be helped and what kind of relief could be given to them;
(b) How the victims of the communal violence shall be rehabilitated;
(c) The kind of compensation to be given to the victims of the communal violence.
(2) The National Council shall advice the State Government as to the assistance to be given to the victims of communal violence.
(3) The National Council shall also perform such other act, which may help to control and contain communal violence and help to give relief and rehabilitation and compensation to the victims of communal violence.
(4) it shall be the duty of the National Council to visit the areas affected by the communal violence as soon as the information of occurrence of such violence is received and to send a report of the situation prevailing in such areas along with its recommendations to the Central Government.</td>
<td>Terms and Conditions of Members of national Council

Powers and functions of National Council</td>
</tr>
</table>

	48. The National Council shall, from time to time, submit reports to the Central Government recommending the steps required to be taken to deal with the situation giving rights to communal violence.	Report of National Council
District Council to function under State Council	**CHAPTER IX** **FUNDS FOR RELIEF AND REHABILITATION**	
	49.(1) Every State Government establish a Fund to be called the State Communal Disturbance Relief and Rehabilitation Fund and there shall be credited thereto- (a) all moneys received from the Central Government;	State Fund
Compensation to victims	(b) all moneys received from the State Government; (c) all moneys received by way of gifts or donations, from a public sector undertaking or a local authority or an individual or a private voluntary organization for all or any of the purposes of this Act;	
	(d) amounts received as aid from the international organizations or organizations in India, where necessary, in terms of the existing regulations governing such aid, for the rehabilitation or welfare of victims of communal violence.	45 of 1860
	(2) The Fund shall be applied for the following purposes, namely:- (a) for the purposes of grants for relief and rehabilitation as provided under section 40 and 42; (b) for meeting the expenses for exercising or performing other powers and functions of the Council under section 40, and (c) for such other purposes as may be prescribed; (3) The State Council shall submit an annual report to the National Council to review the implementation of the orders passed by the courts with regard to awarding of compensation to victims of communal violence.	
Scheme for grant of relief	50.(1) Every State Government shall, by notification, make a scheme for providing funds for the purpose of grant for immediate compensation to the victims or their dependents in the event of loss of life or injury, as the case may be, or to those who have suffered loss or damage to property or loss of means of livelihood or as a result of an offence under the provisions of this Act. (2) The scheme shall be administered by the District Council.	
District Fund	51. Every State Government shall establish a Fund to be called the Victims Assistance Fund in each district and placed the same at the disposal of the District Council and there shall be credited	
		12 of 1855

	52. The District Council in a State shall function under the overall supervision and directions of the State Council. Thereto- a. all monies received from the State Government; b. all monies received by way of gifts or donations from a public or private sector undertakings or a local authority or an individual or a voluntary organization for any or all the purpose of this Act. 52. The District Council in a State shall function under the overall supervision and directions of the State Council. **CHAPTER X** **COMPENSATION TO VICTIMS** 53.(1) Whenever a Special Court convicts a person for an offence punishable under this Act, it may, by its sentence, also pass an order that the offender shall make such monetary compensation as may be specified therein to the person mentioned in sub-section(5) for any loss or damage arising from such offence: Provided that no such compensation shall be awarded to a person who is involved in any offence committed under the Indian Penal ode as specified in the schedule. (2) The amount of compensation shall be such as is determined by the Special Court and be equitable, having regard to the provisions of sub-section(4). (3) An order under sub-section(1) may be made in addition to any other punishment to the which the person convicted is sentenced or where the offence is punishable with fine only, or with imprisonment for a period not exceeding three months, such order may be in lieu of any other punishment. (4) Before passing any order under sub-section(1) the Special Court shall take into consideration the nature of the offence, the motive therefore, the economic status of the offender and the person in whose favor such order is made and all other relevant factors. (5) The compensation awarded under sub-section(1) may be directed to be paid- a) to any person who has incurred expenses in prosecution or defraying any other expenses properly incurred; b) to any person for any loss, damage or injury caused by the offence, when the compensation therefore is , in the opinion of the Special Court, recoverable by such person in a civil court: c) in the case of a conviction for any offence for having caused the death of another person or of having abetted the commission of such offence to the person who are, under the Fatal Accidents Act,1855, entitled to recover damages from the person sentenced, for the loss resulting to themfrom such death;	Immediate compensation

Power of Central Government to give directions to State Government and issue notifications etc.

d) in the case of a conviction for any offence which includes theft, criminal misappropriation, criminal breach of trust, or cheating, robbery, dacoit, extortion or of having dishonestly received or retained, or having voluntarily assisted in disposing of stolen property knowing or having reason to believe the same to be stolen to any bana fide purchaser of such property for the loss of the same, if such property is restored to the possession of the person entitled thereto.

(6) At the time of awarding compensation in any subsequent civil suit relating to the same matter, the court shall take into account any sum paid or recovered as compensation under this section.

54.(1) The District Council shall entertain claims by or on behalf of persons affected by Communal Violence and the District Council shall decide the quantum of immediate compensation to be awarded to the victim or his dependents, as the case may be, after due inquiry within a period of one month from the date of the claim.

(2) The amount of compensation shall not be less than twenty percent of the full rate of compensation as prescribed under each category of cases.

(3) The compensation shall be disbursed to the victim after adjusting any amount of assistance he might have received under any other scheme of the State Government for grant of relief or compensation.

(4) The assistance from the District Fund may not be given to those victims or to the legal heirs if the victim is involved in the Commission of any offence under the provisions of this Act.

CHAPTER XI
SPECIAL POWEROF THE CENTRAL GOVERNMENT TO DEAL WITH COMMUNAL VIOLENCE IN CERTAIN CASES

55.(1) whenever the Central Government is of the opinion that one or more scheduled offences are being committed in any area within a State by any person or group of persons in such manner and on such a scale which involves the use of criminal force or violence against the members of any group, caste or community resulting in death or destruction of property and such use of criminal force or violence is committed with a view to create disharmony or feelings of enmity, hatred, ill will between different groups, castes or communities and there is an imminent threat to the secular fabric, unity, integrity or internal security of India which reuires that immediate steps shall be taken by the State

	Government concerned, it shall- a. draw the attention of the State Government to the prevailing situation in that area; and b. direct the State Government to take all immediate measures to suppress each violence on the issue of a direction under sub-section(1) (2) The State Government shall take appropriate action to prevent and control communal violence on the issue of a direction under sub-section(1) (3) Where the Central Government is of the opinion that the directions issued under sub-section(2) are not followed, it may take such action as is necessary including- a. the issue of a notification declaring any area within a State as "communally disturbed area"; b. the deployment of armed forces, to prevent and control communal violence, on a request having been received from the State Government to do so. (4) Where it is decided to deploy armed forces under sub-section(3), the Central Government or the State Government may constitute an authority to be known as Unified command for the purpose of coordinating and monitoring the role and responsibilities of the forces of the Union and States and for giving appropriate directions to such forces. (5) The forces deployed under sub-section(3) shall act under the control and as per the directions of the District Magistrate or any officer nominated by the State Government or the Unified Command. Every notification issued by the Central Government under clause(a) of sub-section(3) shall be laid before each House of Parliament.	There to from such death; Government concerned, it shall section(1)]
Power of Central Government to extend or modify notifications issued under section 55	56.(1) A notification under section 55 shall specify the period for which the area shall remain so notified: Provided that the period specified under such notification shall not, in the first instance, exceed thirty days: Provided further that the Central Government may extend the said period, by notification, if in its opinion the area continues to be a communally disturbed area: Provided also that the total period during which an area may be notified as a communally disturbed area shall not exceed a total continuous period of sixty days. (2) Where the Central Government is satisfied that such disturbance of public peace and tranquility as is referred to in sub-section(1) no longer persists in such area, it shall amend the notification issued in respect of that area to limit the period specified therein[whether originally or by amendment under sub-section(1)]	

CHAPTER XII
POWERS, DUTIES AND IMMUNITIES OF THE OFFICERS

Protection of action taken in good faith

57.(1) No suit, prosecution or other legal proceedings shall lie against the State Government, the Central Government or any officer or authority of such Government or any other person or any member of the State Council, National or District Council for anything which is in good faith done or intended to be done under this Act or the rules made thereunder.

(2) It shall be the duty of the State Government or the Central Government, as the case may be, to provide required legal aid to an officer or authority facing a suit or legal proceeding in terms of sub-section(1)

(3) An officer or authority of the State Government or the Central Government who suffers an injury or is killed in the discharge of his duty while acting under the provisions of this Act shall be given special compensation or ex gratia relief at double the rate of such compensation or ex gratia relief as is admissible in respect of other Government servants on duty in terms of the existing rules or guidelines framed by the State Government or the Central Government, as the case may be.

CHAPTER XIII
MISCELLANEOUS

Prohibition against discrimination

58. while providing compensation and relief to the victims of communal violence-

(a) there shall be no discrimination on the grounds of sex, caste, community, descent or religion; and

(b) Uniformity of assistance irrespective of caste, community or religion is maintained.

Application of other laws not barred

59. Save as otherwise provided, the provisions of this Act shall be in addition to, and not in derogation of, any other laws for the time being in force except to the extent the provisions of other laws are inconsistent with the provisions of this Act.

Power of Central Government to make rules.

60.(1) The Central Government may, by notification, make rules for carrying out the provisions of this Act.

(2) In particular, and without prejudice to the generality of the foregoing power, such rules may provide for all or any of the following matters, namely:-

a) the traveling and other allowances payable to the Members of the National Council under sub-section(1) of section 46;

b) any other matter which is required to be, or may be, prescribed by the Central Government.

	(3) Every rules made by the Central Government under this Act shall be laid, as soon as may be after it is made, before each House of Parliament, while it is in session, for a total period of thirty days which may be comprised in one session or in two or more successive sessions, and if, before the expiry of the session immediately following the session or the successive sessions aforesaid, both Houses agree in making any modification in the rule or both Houses agree that the rule should not be made, the rule shall thereafter have affect only in such modified form or be of no effect, as the case may be; so, however, that any such modification or annulments shall be without prejudice to the validity of anything previously done under that rule. 61.(1) The State Government may, by notification in the Official Gazette, makes rules for carrying out the purposes of this Act, (2) In particular and without prejudice to the generality of the foregoing power, such rules may provide for all or any of the following matters, namely- (a) the term of members appointed under clauses(g) and (h) of section 39; (b) the procedure to be followed by the State Council while performing its functions under sub-section(2) of section 40; (c) the number of members if its District Council and such other Departments which may be represented by the district level officers in the District Council under clause(d) of sub-section(2) of section 42; (d) the terms and conditions of appointment of members under clauses(e) and (f) of sub-section(2) of section 42; (e) the other purposes for which the State fund shall be applied under clause© of sub-section(2) of section 49; (f) any other matter which is required to be, or may be prescribed. (3) Every notification, rule and scheme made under this Act shall be laid, as soon as may be after it is made, before each House of State Legislature where it consists of two Houses, or where such Legislature consists f one House, before that House.	Power of State Government to make rules.
	62. In the Representation of the People At,1951, in section 8, in sub-section(2), after clause©, the following clause shall be inserted, namely:- "Any provision of the Communal Violence (Prevention, Control and Rehabilitation of Victims) Act, 2005"	Amendment of section 8 of Act 43 of 1951.

THE SCHEDULE

[See Clause(I) of sub-section(I) of section 2]

1. Offences under the following provisions of the Indian Penal Code(45 of 1860):-

   Sections 120B, 143, 144, 145, 14 , 148, 150, 151, 152, 153, 153A, 153B, 154, 155, 156, 157, 158, 160, 295, 295, 296, 297, 298, 302, 303, 304, 304, 307, 308, 323, 234, 325, 326, 327 to 335, 341 to 348, 352, 353, 354, 355 to 358, 363 to 369, 376, 379, 380, 383, 384 to 387, 392, 402, 411, 412, 426, 427, 431, 435, 436, 440, 447 to 462, 504 to 506 and 509.
2. Offences under the following provisions of the Arms Act, 1959(54 of 1959):Sections 25,26,27,28 to 30.
3. Offences under the following provisions of the Explosives Act,1884:Sections 6(3), 8(2) and 9B.
4. Offences under the following provisions of the Prevention of Damage to public Property Act, 1984(3 of 1984)- Sections 3 and 4.
5. Offence under the following provisions of the places of Worship (Special Provisions) Act, 1991(42 of 1991)-Section 6.
6. Offences under the following provisions of the Religious Institutions (Prevention of Misuse) Act,1988(41 of 1988)-Section7.

STATEMENT OF OBJECTS AND REASONS

Communal violence threatens the secular fabric, unity, integrity and internal security of a nation. With a view to empowering the State Governments and the Central Government to take effective measures to provide for the prevention and control of communal violence and to rehabilitate the victims of such violence, for speedy investigation and trial of offences including imposition of enhanced punishments, than those provided in the Indian Penal Code, on persons involved in communal violence and for that matters connected there with, it has been decided to enact a law by Parliament.

2. The Bill, inter alia, seeks to-
   i. Provide for declaration of certain areas as communally disturbed areas by the State Governments;
   ii. Lay down measures for prevention of acts leading to communal violence; Enhance punishments for offences relating to communal violence for certain other offences;
   iii. Makes provisions for speedy investigation and trial of offences through Special Courts;
   iv. Make institutional arrangements for relief and rehabilitation measures for victims of communal violence;
   v. Make provisions for the compensation to the victims of communal violence and provide for special powers to the Central Government in certain cases;
   vi. Provide for constitution of a National Communal Disturbance Relief and Rehabilitation Council, State Communal Disturbance Relief and Rehabilitation Council and District
   vii. Communal Disturbance Relief and Relief and rehabilitation Council;
   viii. Prohibit any discrimination in providing compensation and relief to the victims of the communal violence on grounds of sex, caste, community or religion.
3. The Notes on clauses explain in detail the various provisions contained in the Bill.
4. The Bill seeks to achieve the above objects.

ENVIRONMENT

Nowadays we see the difference where animals are living and where we are living. Isn't it a shame? First we cleared forests, destroyed habitats of several species then converted forest land into residential areas, then put every effort in polluting, and at last we go to higher reaches for trekking, hiking, and camping to find some mental peace and enjoy in a pollution free zone. We are using our environment in such a sense that there is no more tomorrow or there will be no generations to come. We make sure that we can extract every bit of it for us, but in replay we do not even think of giving it something so that some people who will succeed us will remember us for our goodness. Our environment says us that "I am a faithful servant but a delicate one, if handled properly, I will give lifelong service". The pressure of increasing population, growth of industries, urbanization, energy intensive life style, loss of forest cover, lack of environmental awareness, lack of implementation of environmental rules and regulations and environment improvement plans, untreated effluent discharge from industries and municipalities, use of non-biodegradable pesticides/fungicides/ herbicides/insecticides, use of chemical fertilizers instead of organic manures, etc. are causing water pollution. The pollutants from industrial discharge and sewage besides finding their way to surface water reservoirs and rivers are also percolating into ground to pollute ground water sources. The polluted water may have undesirable color, odor, taste, turbidity, organic matter contents, harmful chemical contents, toxic and heavy metals, pesticides, oily matters, industrial waste products, radioactivity, high Total Dissolved Solids (TDS), acids,

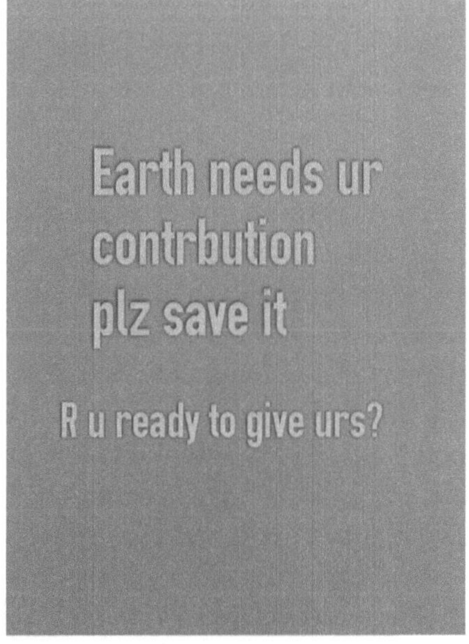

alkaline, domestic sewage content, virus, bacteria, protozoa, rotifers, worms, etc. The organic content may be biodegradable or non-biodegradable. Pollution of surface waters (rivers, lakes, ponds), ground waters, sea water are all harmful for human and animal health. Pollution of the drinking water and that of the food chain is by far the most worrisome aspect.

Can you please tell me any component of our environment, which we have not polluted? I am not going to define the various pollutions here, that everyone knows, but nobody cares. The main problem is our mentality, the problem of "NONE OF MY BUSINESS". We will throw our wastes all around by simply thinking that "municipality people will come, they are paid for this,why should we care". This attitude is to be changed right now, otherwise it will be too late. We have to take active participation in keeping our environment clean. Recently our PM Shri Narendra Modi has launched a campaign regarding cleanliness, i.e. Swatch Bharat Abhiyan. Its main theme was to clean your own surroundings and mainly dispose your wastes in a proper way, make use of dustbins, do not pollute public places. Though it was accepted by all states but its real result will come if our mentality gets changed. If we generate the feeling of considering our surroundings as our own house, we know that if we are not going to pollute our environment, nobody has the power to make it polluted.

Intentionally or unintentionally, we have polluted the air, water, and soil. With the result, how many species became extinct or are on the verge of extinction? Only man is responsible of extinction of species, except man who else is polluting environment? Give me only one name of any living creature. If we look, all living creatures are family members of our earth, whether aquatic or terrestrial, as like in our home. Suppose if any member of family, say brother or sister, will pollute our house in any form or simply will turn off the AC in a hot climate, what will be our reaction? We will simply throw him out. Now look at it in a broader sense, aren't we making the life horrible for our other members? Have we once thought of that?

If any animal harms us, we simply say "kill this wild animal", but what about tens of thousands of species which suffer every minute because of us? Our school was situated near farms with lush green landscapes. During our school days, there were numerous snakes roaming around, but all were non-poisonous. Sometimes we used to catch them in bottles. On average, we used to see forty to fifty snakes every day during summers. But today after only fifteen years, I can hardly find any one by walking kilometers in that area. One day I thought, where have they gone? I want to play with them again, putting them in bottles or my school bag, chasing them. But tears fell from my eyes, missing them and that life. Finally I came to know it was due to the fertilizers they got extinct. Now the people who work in fields hardly see any. Now tell me who is responsible, who is to be punished, can we bring them back? They have suffered because of our greediness and selfishness.

Our duty finishes after cleaning our house and then throwing the wastes outside. We only consider our house our own not the whole environment. When this feeling changes, our whole environment will be neat and clean, free from pollution. There will be no suffering of other species, no extinction, nothing. Now we will have a look of different kinds of pollutions and their causes, effects and remedial actions to reverse the situation:

Category	Major causes	Major symptoms
Atmospheric pollution	Smoke, dust, exhaust fumes, toxic substances (such as sulfur dioxide and nitrogen dioxide)	Asthma, bronchitis
Water pollution	Polluted waste water, waste fluids (such as petroleum), sludge, household sewage, sewage discharge, general waste, agricultural chemicals	Noxious odors, poisoning

Category	Major causes	Major symptoms
Soil pollution	Arsenic, heavy metals (especially in agricultural chemicals)	
Noise	Factories, construction work, road traffic, trains and aircraft, late-night commercial operations, advertising	Headaches, insomnia, depression, hearing loss, impaired development
Vibration	Factories, construction work, road traffic, trains and aircraft	Dizziness, discomfort, structural damage to homes
Ground subsidence	Up swelling of groundwater, gravel quarrying, coal mining	Structural damage to buildings
Noxious odors	Exhaust fumes, river contamination, sanitation facilities, accumulated sewage, livestock farms, etc.	Headaches, discomfort

Now recapitulate the different pollutions, sources, and related problems we cause on a daily basis whether intentionally or intentionally. We should wake up and join our hands at all levels to make our earth like a paradise not a hell to live in. It is only in our hands, we have to do it as simply we are tempering it. This is Mother Earth, not a dustbin.

WATER POLLUTION

Surface waters may have the following types of pollutions:

(a) Suspended solids: The inorganic suspended solids blanket the stream bed effecting benthos (flora and fauna at bottom of water) organisms, while the organic solids create sludge banks and decompose causing odors and pathogens.

(b) Floating solids including oils, greases: Floating materials obstruct passage of light and aeration which are vital for flora and fauna and self-purification of water.
(c) Organic matter: Biological decomposition of waste organic matter in stream depletes dissolved oxygen content of water which may stifle the fish and aquatic life due to lack of oxygen. Unpleasant odor, flavor and taste, result due to lack of dissolved oxygen. Untreated sewage is the biggest pollutant and a cause of pathogens in water.
(d) Inorganic dissolved salts: High total dissolved solids (TDS) may interfere with the use of water in industries, municipal supplies and for irrigation purposes. Phosphorus and Nitrogen are plant nutrients which induce algae growth and sometimes create 'Eutrophic' condition when excessive plant and algal growth may kill fishes and water animals.
(e) Acid, alkalies, toxic chemicals and heavy metals: Adverse effect on human and animal life and plants.
(f) Radioactive materials: Adverse effects on all biological beings.
(g) Foam and color are indicators of contaminations.
(h) Microorganisms: Pathogenic bacteria, viruses, etc are health hazards.
(i) Thermal pollution: Heat depletes dissolved oxygen in water adversely affecting fishes. Higher temperature of water also adversely effects its use as coolant in industries.

Ground waters may also have some of the pollutants mentioned in case of surface waters such as heavy metals, high total dissolved solids (TDS), high salinity or solidity, fluoride, arsenic, nitrates denoting organic pollution, pesticides, radioactivity, bad odors and flavor, color, pathogens, etc.

CARCINOGENS IN WASTE WATER

Wastes from certain industries or leakages of certain materials in handling, processing, etc. may have substances which can cause cancer in humans or animals. These carcinogenic substances may find their way in waste waters which may pollute the source of waters for general use. Many of the heavy and toxic metals (like nickel, chromium), radioactive substances, certain dyes, inks, resins, fumigants, gasoline additives, nitro phenyl, naphthyamines, benzamine, azo compounds, some of the pesticides like D.D.T. etc. are carcinogens. Smoke from combustion of certain organic materials may contain carcinogens which may eventually find their way to pollute waters, besides polluting air.

Prevention from exposure, removal of such compounds or breaking down of such compounds should be attempted.

POLLUTION BY E-WASTE

India generated about 1050 tons of electronic scrap per year as reported in April 2005 which increased to 146,000 tons of e-waste per year as reported in May 2007. This would go on increasing year by year. A study by U.S. environmental protection agency shows that e-waste forms about 1% of municipal solid waste in USA. California alone discards 6000 computers daily. They have estimated that about 70% of heavy metals found in the landfills there, come from electronic discards which may contaminate ground waters. When e-waste is incinerated with other wastes it leads to hazardous emission-containing 'Dioxins'. The commonly found metals in e-waste like copper are catalyst for 'Dioxin' formation.

SOURCES OF WATER POLLUTANTS

Effluents and solid wastes from various industries and municipalities, indiscriminate use of toxic chemicals, indiscriminate use of pesticides, insecticides and fungicides, leaching of soils, wastes and rocks are the principal causes of water pollution. Objectionable level of pollution of water due to oils and oily substances may be found mainly in surface waters near the industries using heavy quantities of lubricating oils, greases, and liquid fuels, or refineries, big oil storages, etc. Ground water may also be polluted due to soaking of oil in the ground or by indiscriminate disposal of oil sludge. The heaviest polluting source for surface water is sewage from cities.

AIR POLLUTION

All around the earth there is a thick blanket of air called the atmosphere. Air, like other gases, does not have a fixed shape. It spreads out to fill any available space so nothing is really empty. But air cannot escape from the atmosphere as the force of gravity keeps it from floating away from the earth.

Ever since people first gathered in settlements there has been pollution. Pollution usually refers to the presence of substances that are either present in the environment where it doesn't belong or at levels greater than it should be.

Air pollution is caused by any undesirable substance, which enters the atmosphere. Air pollution is a major problem in modern society. Even though air pollution is usually a greater problem in cities, pollutants contaminate air everywhere. These substances include various gases and tiny particles, or particulates that can harm human health and damage the environment. They may be gases, liquids, or solids. Many pollutants are given off into the air as a result of human behavior. Pollution occurs on different levels: personal, national, and global.

Some pollutants come from natural sources.

- Forest fires emit particulates, gases, and VOCs (substances that vaporize into the atmosphere)
- Ultra-fine dust particles created by soil erosion when water and weather loosen layers of soil, increase airborne particulate levels
- Volcanoes spew out sulfur dioxide and large amounts of pulverized lava rock known as volcanic ash

The major types of air pollution are:

Gaseous pollutants: A different mix of vapors and gaseous air pollutants is found in outdoor and indoor environments. The most common gaseous pollutants are carbon dioxide, carbon monoxide, hydrocarbons, nitrogen oxides, sulfur oxides and ozone. A number of sources produce these chemical compounds but the major manmade source is the burning of fossil fuel. Indoor air pollution is caused by cigarette smoking, the use of certain construction materials, cleaning products, and home furnishings. Outdoor gaseous pollutants come from volcanoes, fires, and industry, and in some areas may be substantial. The most commonly recognized type of air pollution is smog. Smog generally refers to a condition caused by the action of sunlight on exhaust gases from motor vehicles and factories.

Greenhouse effect prevents the sun's heat from rising out of the atmosphere and flowing back into space. This warms the earth's surface causing the greenhouse effect. While a certain amount of greenhouse gases in the atmosphere are necessary to make the earth warm, activities such as the burning of fossil fuels are creating a gaseous layer that is too dense to allow the heat to escape. Many scientists believe this is causing global warming. Other gases contributing to the problem include chlorofluorocarbons (CFC), methane, nitrous oxides, and ozone.

Acid rain forms when moisture in the air interacts with nitrogen oxide and sulfur dioxide released by factories, power plants, and motor vehicles that burn coal or oil. This interaction of gases with water vapor forms sulfuric acid and nitric acids. Eventually these chemicals fall to earth as precipitation, or acid rain. Acid rain pollutants may travel long distances, with winds carrying them thousands of miles before they fall as dew, drizzle, fog, snow or rain.

Damage to the ozone layer is primarily caused by the use of chlorofluorocarbons (CFCs). Ozone is a form of oxygen found in the earth's upper atmosphere. The thin layer of ozone molecules in the atmosphere absorb some of the sun's ultraviolet (UV) rays before it reaches the earth's surface, making life on earth possible. The depletion of ozone is causing higher levels of UV radiation on earth, endangering both plants and animals.

Particulate matter is the general term used for a mixture of solid particles and liquid droplets found in the air. Some particles are large or dark enough to be seen as soot or smoke. Others are so small they can be detected only with an electron microscope. When particulate matter is breathed in, it can irritate and damage the lungs causing breathing problems. Fine particles are easily inhaled deeply into the lungs where they can be absorbed into the blood stream or remain embedded for long periods of time.

Climatic effects: Normally pollutants rise or flow away from their sources without building up to unsafe levels. Wind patterns, clouds, rain, and temperature can affect how quickly pollutants move away from an area. Weather patterns that can trap air pollution in valleys or move it across the globe may be able to damage pristine environments far from the original sources.

How does air pollution affect me?

Many studies have shown links between pollution and health effects. Increases in air pollution have been linked to decreases in lung function and increases in heart attacks. High levels of air pollution according to the EPA Air Quality Index directly affect people with asthma and other types of lung or heart disease. Overall air quality has improved in the last 20 years but urban areas are still a concern. The elderly and children are especially vulnerable to the effects of air pollution.

The level of risk depends on several factors:

- the amount of pollution in the air,
- the amount of air we breathe in a given time
- our overall health.

Other, less direct ways people are exposed to air pollutants are:

- eating food products contaminated by air toxins that have been deposited where they grow,
- Drinking water contaminated by air pollutants,
- ingesting contaminated soil, and
- touching contaminated soil, dust or water.

NOISE POLLUTION

Noise is one of the most pervasive pollutant. A musical clock may be nice to listen during the day, but may be an irritant during sleep at night. Noise by definition is "sound without value" or "any nose that is unwanted by the recipient". Noise in industries such as stone cutting and crushing, steel forgings, loudspeakers, shouting by hawkers selling their wares, movement of heavy transport vehicles, railways and airports leads to irritation and an increased blood pressure, loss of temper, decrease in work efficiency , loss of hearing which may be first temporary but can become permanent in the noise stress continues. It is therefore of utmost importance that excessive noise is controlled. Noise level is measured in terms of decibels (dB). W.H.O. (World Health Organization) has prescribed optimum noise level as 45 dB by day and 35 dB by night. Anything above 80 dB is hazardous.

SOURCES OF NOISE POLLUTION

Noise pollution is a growing problem. All human activities contribute to noise pollution to varying extent. Sources of noise pollution are many and may be located indoors or outdoors.

Indoor sources include noise produced b radio, television, generators, electric fans, air coolers, air conditioners, different home appliances, and family conflict. Noise pollution is more in cities due to a higher concentration of population and industries and activities such as transportation. Noise like other pollutants is a by product of industrialization, urbanization and modern civilization.

Outdoor sources of noise pollution include indiscriminate use of loudspeakers, industrial activities, automobiles, rail traffic, aero planes and activities such as those at market place, religious, social, and cultural functions, sports and political rallies. In rural areas farm machines, pump sets are main sources of noise pollution. During festivals, marriage and many other occasions, use of fire crackers contribute to noise pollution.

EFFECTS OF NOISE POLLUTION

Noise pollution is highly annoying and irritating. Noise disturbs sleep, causes hypertension (high blood pressure), emotional problems such as aggression, mental depression and annoyance. Noise pollution adversely affects efficiency and performance of individuals.

PREVENTION AND CONTROL OF NOISE POLLUTION

Following steps can be taken to control or minimize noise pollution-

- Road traffic nose can be reduced by better designing and proper maintenance of vehicles.
- Noise abatement measures include creating noise mounds, noise attenuation walls and well maintenance roads and smooth surfacing of roads.
- Retrofitting of locomotives, continuously welded rail track, use of electric locomotives or deployment of quieter rolling stock will reduce noises emanating from trains.

- Air traffic noise can be reduced by appropriate insulation and introduction of noise regulations for takeoff and landing of aircrafts at the airport.
- Industrial noise can be reduced by sound proofing equipment like generators and areas producing lot of noise.
- Power tools, very loud music and land movers, public functions using loudspeakers etc. should not be permitted at night. Use of horns, alarms, refrigeration units, etc. is to be restricted. Use of fire crackers which are noisy and cause air pollution should be restricted.
- A green belt of trees is an efficient noise absorber.

SOIL POLLUTION

Addition of substances which adversely affect the quality of soil or its fertility is known as soil pollution. Generally polluted water also pollute soil. Solid waste is a mixture of plastics, cloth, glass, metal and organic matter, sewage, sewage sludge, building debris, generated from households, commercial and industries establishments add to soil pollution. Fly ash, iron and steel slag, medical and industrial wastes disposed on land are important source of soil pollution. In addition, fertilizers and pesticides from agricultural use which reach soil as runoff and land filling by municipal waste are growing cause of soil pollution. Acid rain and dry deposition of pollutants on land surface also contribute to soil pollution.

SOURCES OF SOIL POLLUTION

Plastic bags- Plastic bags made from low density polyethylene (LDPE), is virtually indestructible, create colossal environmental hazard. The discarded bags block drains and sewages systems. Leftover food, vegetable waste etc. on which cows and dogs feed may die due to the choking by plastic bags. Plastic is non-biodegradable and burning of plastic in garbage dumps release highly toxic and poisonous gases like carbon monoxide, carbon dioxide, phosgene, dioxins and other poisonous chlorinated compounds.

Industrial sources – It includes fly ash, chemical residues, metallic and nuclear wastes. Large number of industrial chemicals, dyes, acids, etc. find their way into the soil and are known to create many health hazards including cancer.

Agricultural sources – Agricultural chemicals especially fertilizers and pesticides pollute the soil. Fertilizers in the runoff water from these fields can cause eutrophication in water bodies. Pesticides are highly toxic chemicals which affect humans and other animals adversely causing respiratory problems, cancer and death.

CONTROL OF SOIL POLLUTION

Indiscriminate disposal of solid waste should be avoided.

To control soil pollution, it is essential to stop the use of plastic bags and instead use bags of degradable materials like paper and cloth. Sewage should be treated properly before using as fertilizer and as landfills. The organic matter from domestic, agricultural and other waste should be segregated and subjected to vermicomposting which generates useful manure as a byproduct. The industrial wastes prior to disposal should be properly treated for removing hazardous materials. Biomedical waste should be separately collected and incinerated in proper incinerators.

This was one side of a coin, now look at the other side: there are people who are really exceptional and marvelous. They are very noble and their work should be appreciated and we should follow their path. They are also among us, but due to their selfless work they stay above us. These people really need more support and a grand salute from all of us. They simply believe in humanity and do not have any caste, religion, creed etc. Now I will mention some of them here by name as we should learn from their exceptional work towards our society. These people are really morally sound as far my opinion is considered. They are examples for everyone. Have a look at them and their deeds.

Attaullah Sharieff Shahtaj Khadari baba is popularly known as Biryani baba. For forty years, he has been serving biryani to the poor in Andhra Pradesh's Krishna district. He is a religious man and is continuing the legacy of his guru baba who passed away forty years ago. He says that he offers meals daily to the needy. With the help of devotees and donors, the program is running smoothly.

Around one thousand people come for seeking blessings from him daily and on special occasions the number goes up to 8000–10000. On an average around two tons of basmati rice and quintals of mutton and chicken and pure ghee are needed for making biryani. Vegetarian food is also available. The food is served in Cheemalpadu Dargah's premises in Langar Khana. His main aim is to serve food to poor people, be they of any religion.

There is a school for grannies too. It is open for just two hours a day and the uniform is pink sarees. At Aajibaichi Shala the students are aged sixty to ninety. Set up by Motiram Dalal and Yogendra Bangar, this school is located in Phangane Thane and is the first school for grandmothers who are uneducated. This school was started for inculcating respect and love for elderly, said the founder. Yogendra Bangar says that they are encouraged by everyone in the school. "We have done something like this for the first time and this is definitely good for our society. Knowledge is a very important thing in life and educating these elderly people is extremely essential. This school was started for bringing happiness to the lives of elderly."

Udaipur's "Shloka Beti Garden" would give relatives and parents a chance for celebrating the birth of girl and that too by planting one sapling. This dream of Devendra Agarwal is being fulfilled by workers and construction work is on in full swing. This garden would celebrate the daughter's birthday. Soon two acres of land on Tiger Hill would be converted to "Shloka Beti Garden" wherein relatives and parents would be given a chance for celebrating the joy. Devendra said that currently the society is prejudiced and some people still prioritize sons over daughters. At this garden, people would realize that the difference between girls and boys doesn't exist. Girls would be welcomed with love and dignity.

Meena Mehta and her husband Atul from Surat are making a lot of difference to the health and personal hygiene of underprivileged girls in the city. Sanitary napkins and hygienic kits are distributed by them in schools and neighborhood. Girls always feel happy and thankful to them after receiving this. Each kit contains one bar of soap, four sachets of shampoo, two sets of undergarments and one sanitary napkin packet. These free kits are distributed once a month in one school for the hearing- and visually-impaired, one school for blind and twenty two municipal schools. Apart from school children, these kits are distributed to women in her neighborhood too, such as daughters of watchmen, vegetable sellers and housemaids. A unique thing is that she has made a rule of absentees not getting the kits, due to which the attendance is improved greatly. Her main intention is that girls must remain clean and shouldn't catch infections. About one lakh is spent by them on this and the initiative is completely self-funded. Hats off to the couple!

For this man, there is only one religion and that is humanity. He doesn't believe in any other religion. Being eighty three years old, Mithalal Sindhi is from Ahmedabad and for sixty years, he has been living on the footpath. He adds that he is absolutely satisfied with whatever life has given him. He has done something for the city's people which would always be remembered. People respect him for this. For fifty seven years now, Mithalal is doing an act which is purely symbolic of social service and incredible selflessness. He performs the last rites of dead bodies that aren't claimed by anyone. You won't believe, but it is true that until now, he has performed the last rites of around 550 unclaimed bodies.

For Melghat, the most malnourished area of Maharashtra, Dr. Ravindra Kolhe is surely a blessing. He has spread a lot of medical awareness in the area, which has brought down infant mortality rate from 200 per 1000 to just 60. He has been working there for three decades now and charge just two rupees for medical consultation and support from his wife Smita who is also a doctor.

Apart from this, the couple is involved in spreading awareness about the education and health of women. No government aid would be accepted by him since he believes in self-reliance, however he accepted several awards bestowed upon him. Hats off to the efforts put in by him and his wife.

This man, through his death, gave life to four critically ill patients who were awaiting transplants. Eighteen-year-old Deepak Dhaketa, a newspaper vendor in Indore, whom the doctors declared as brain dead, saving four people. All four organs, two kidneys, liver, and heart was transplanted successfully, after his family agreed for the same. Within the city, three green corridors were created for transporting the organs. All organs were successfully transplanted, according to the doctors.

While kidneys were transplanted in two patients at Choithram Hospital and SAIMS, both in Indore, his heart and liver were flown to Delhi. While the heart recipient was a forty eight year old women who suffered from end-stage heart disease, the liver receiver was a fifty year old man who suffered from liver failure. Transporting these organs was definitely a very big challenge.

Free food is being offered by Mumbai couples to these needy ones, however, once you know the cause of this, you are definitely going to be in tears. Yes, Mr. and Mrs. Tanna are doing something which would definitely touch your heart. They lost their twenty seven year old son named Nimesh in an unexpected accident. They were completely disheartened when they lost their one and only son. After their son's demise, they had to face one more tragedy as they lost their Mulund's sweet shop after the partner cheated them. Owing to this motivation and the helping hand offered by the best friend of their son, Kintan, they were able to start a new shop. There was a gradual improvement in their economic status and so, they took the decision of helping the needy in the name of their son. It started off as SNTCT, Shri Nimesh Tanna Charitable Trust on 26 January 2013. Free tiffin was prepared for around thirty people, taking the help of dabbawalas who look after the delivery. Apart from this, a food kit is provided that has flour, sugar, oil, and grains etc. for tribes. They also have a 'Kids Bank' which supplies cycles, books, toys and clothes.

Akbar Khan has taken a new step towards communal harmony. This resident of Jaipur has built a Shiva temple which spreads over one hundred square meters in Om Vihar Colony. He had never faced any objection from anyone. He has stated that for him Ram and Allah both are same. He is of the opinion that both religions must be respected equally. Basically, Akbar Khan had a good connection to Lord Shiva and this faith had come naturally. He claimed that every time some problem was encountered, he would offer prayers to Shiva. After this, all his troubles would disappear. So he took the decision of dedicating this temple, which he built himself without any financial help. However, this isn't all. Before opening 'Bhooteshwar Mahadev' temple on April 30, invitation prayers of Lord Ganpati was organized by Mr. Khan. Also a kalash yatra was organized including 251 women, who would participate in a yagna.

This lady police officer, named Luisa Fernaada Urrea has done such a thing which would definitely teach you something. She has saved a life, but in a very different way which you can never imagine.

An infant was found starving to death in Colombia's jungles and this woman breastfed her. It was reported that paramedics took too long to arrive, when that lady cop came across her. The cop is a mother and she couldn't see the new-born girl in misery and hence, she took the decision of feeding her right away. The infant is being taken care of until some adoptive center is found. Currently the officer is posted in Colombia's La Marina.

Khor's shopping center has set up a refrigerated shelf which is stuffed with food. This food can be picked up only by the unemployed or people who don't have cash. The instructions are written on the shelf in English and Arabic languages which read "free food only for people who are unemployed or don't have cash". This initiative was praised by a cross section of people, suggesting also that local charities could come forward and help these shopping outlets for launching these shelves. People are of the opinion that hypermarkets, malls and restaurants must have these shelves as it is a humanitarian and thoughtful gesture.

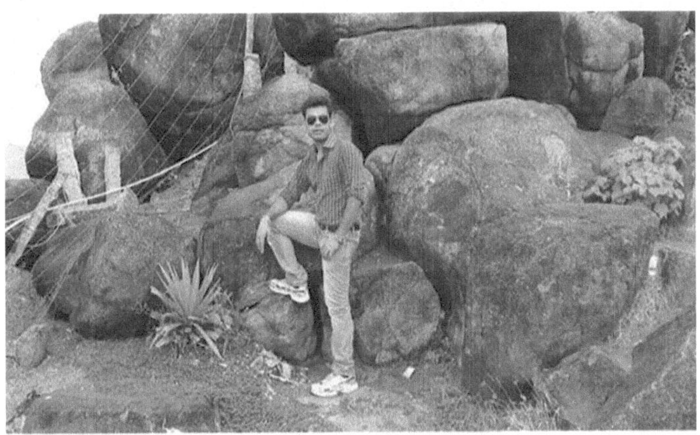

He is Rajesh, a brave citizen of India, who cares for the safety and modesty of women and raises his voice to defend them. Without a second thought, he stood like a wall to save the dignity of a girl who was traveling with him in a train from Dehradun to Delhi.

There were two passengers who were misbehaving with her as she was traveling alone in an overnight train. Mr. Rajesh gave them several warnings but they didn't stop, continuing to harass the girl using unconstitutional language, and taking pictures. And instead of stopping they threatened Mr. Rajesh to stay quiet. Mr. Rajesh was so bold and courageous that he was ready to face anything all alone. He soon informed the police and the culprits were arrested. We salute this gentlemen for his act of bravery and hope others also take a cue from him which will help make India a safer place for women.

Today Kali Bein's river bed is a delight to watch, thanks to the efforts of Sant Balbir Singh Seechewal. Earlier, it was completely filled with garbage and filth, unless he took the responsibility to himself. Popular by the name "eco baba", he along with several volunteers took the decision of taking the entire responsibility of cleaning. Apart from cleaning, some dry parts were rejuvenated. The banks were completely beautified as many trees were planted. Since the water flow is now restored, thousands of hectares of land are being reclaimed from water-logging in Hoshiarpur District's Tehsil Dasuya, from Kapurthala district's desertification as well as Mand areas' flood. He along with his team ensured that people around that area were taught about disadvantages of dumping garbage and waste in the river.

Pavithra and her husband Ashok have changed lives of 1500 disabled and challenged people. She set up a BPO, namely

Vindhya, which gives employment only to disabled people. Her first step was taking an office space and then putting a board outside that said, 'only physically challenged people will be employed'. Communication with people who were deaf and dumb happened purely through pen and paper. Now, they entertain big clients like Wipro, SAP , Yes bank, Indus land bank, etc. However, these clients came in only after some processes were brought in by Pavitra for quick TATs. Recently, transgendered individuals are also hired by this BPO. Extensive training is carried out in the form of Braille sessions, sign language etc. They have a separate HR department to assess skills of people. Now, the services are extended to loan processing, document management, voice and non-voice process, digitalization and data conversion.

Sheikh Abdul mateen, a math's teacher by profession is providing 8000–10000 litters of free water daily to around 200 families in latur, from his bore well. He himself sits there for around 4 hours and offers water to needy people. He states that during his house's construction work, he dug a bore well and by the grace of God, water was found. Since severe water crisis is being witnessed in the area, around 200 families come to him for collected bore well water. He is very kind and generous person .helping people is his hobby we must definitely appreciate this act of sheikh Abdul mateen.

What he does for children is truly worth appreciating and is an inspiration for all. Brijendra has retired from the army and now he is a security guard in Majra's Allahabad bank ATM. In the evening, he gathers children who are forced into begging and child labor, in order to teach them. There are around twenty four children who come to learn from him, from nearby slums. He teaches many things including discipline. This duty is being carried out for sixteen years now. We must learn from his acts.

In Harekela's dusty village, there is a man named Hajabba. He has some miraculous contribution towards society and he himself is from a poor family. He has a dream of building a school wherein poor children could come and learn. Hajabba was very poor and he had never been to school. Here is the story of his devotion towards society.

At a very young age, he took up the job of selling oranges. A foreigner came in to buy some oranges from him. They conversed in English and started asking about the price. Since he couldn't speak English , he felt quite ashamed. From that day, he has a clear mjission of setting up a school for poor children. His wife Maimoona often used to complain that he was wasting money which was meant for his own children, but later she realized the importance. In 1999, he started a small school with twenty eight students. Since the number of students started growing, he started accumulating each rupee for building a big school. Then in 2004 he purchased fifty acres of land and realized that the savings were not enough. He sought help from rich individuals and politicians, but no one helped. One day the founder of an organization, Alban Menezes, tried calling him but was shocked to hear from Hajabba's son that Hajabba is hospitalised. Earlier Hajabba refused to comment as to what happened, but after a lot of coaxing he opened up that he was very sad as there was no money to construct his damaged house as he has spent all his savings on school. Alban decided to build a house for Hajabba who has done so much for the society. Now, he is happy and has plans of starting a college.

AWE-INSPIRING DINNER OF MY LIFE

Ladakh :I, along with two friends, went to Ladakh on tour for a week. In Ladakh we went to Pangong Lake which is 170 ks approximately from Leh. A beautiful lake, as no words can describe its beauty and charm. We reached there at 4 pm. We set up a tent on its bank and arranged our items as per our requirement. We were enjoying its charm until the wind came at around 9 pm. The wind was so powerful that it took our tent off the ground. We were so worried about what to do, with no option left except to pass the horrible night in our car. We winded up our all accessories along with that deceased tent and moved towards our car. It was so cold at that time, we were shivering with the cold.

A lady of approximately thirty was watching our whole episode, then she came to us and told us that we need not worry at all. She was having her own house there. We hardly knew each other's language but what was graspable was enough for us. She was taking care of shifting us to her house where she was living with her father and mother. We thought for a while but then decided to move. We parked our car in front of her house and quickly moved inside as we were shivering with cold. She alloted us a room and soon offered the famous Ladakhi tea which was much needed for that time to send off the cold. She, along with her mother, took care of us as though we were part of their household. They were such kind and generous people. We had a healthy talk with her mother as she knew our language; she in her childhood days had spent some time in our town, as her father was a policeman and was posted there. In the meanwhile her daughter prepared dinner for us and served it, a memorable dinner really. We were so shocked as we looked at each others' faces; are they really too good? Or was any untoward thing going to happen? We were having suspicions initially that we are among strangers, and they could do anything with us. But it was over after some time and we became so familiar with each other.

On the next day we started to move, and I offered them money ,which later on I felt ashamed of. The lady said, "We are happy what we have, I do only for people in trouble." And she added, "When you come next time, I will charge then, but come again." We thanked them and moved on. After a few kilometers we stopped our car and start memorizing what has happened to us. Are we in our world where humanity is in our dictionaries only. We were speechless. Again, a "thank you" to that noble family. Will see you soon again as we had promised earlier, thank you so much.

I have taken up some small issues with what we are doing and what we are facing. Try to lighten up your inner soul; maybe he will do good for himself and for others. Sometimes, do for others' happiness - it will give you immense pleasure. Wipe tears of someone and I bet someone will come from nowhere to wife yours when you need someone. Make a pledge as we should be remembered as good human beings. We should become role models for others too: in our kindness, honesty, trust, faith. As children we are innocent, loving and honest about our feelings. But as time passes, many social and cultural factors and experiences change our personality and behavior. These experiences often take away some of our honesty and innocence. In the same way, the old way of life was innocent like a child because in those days people were more honest and caring about each other than they are in the busy, modern-day world. When we meet people today, we often do not mean what we say. We only say nice things to them because we don't want to seem rude.

Be soft. Do not let the world make you hard. Do not let pain make you hate. Do not let the bitterness steal your sweetness. Take pride that even though the rest of the world may disagree, you still believe it to be a beautiful place.

Iain S. Thomas

If we have no peace, it is because we have forgotten that we belong to each other.

Mother Teresa

Predators prey on gentleness, peace, calmness, sweetness and any positivity that they sniff out as weakness. Anything that is happy and at peace they mistake for weakness. It's not your job to change these people, but it's your job to show them that your peace and gentleness do not equate to weakness... I compare myself to silk. People mistake silk to be weak but a silk handkerchief can protect the wearer from a gunshot. There are many people who will want to befriend you if you fit the description of what they think is weak; predators want to have friends that they can dominate over because that makes them feel strong and important. The truth is that predators have no strength and no courage. It is you who are strong, and it is you who has courage. I have lost many a friend over the fact that when they attempt to rip me, they can't. They accuse me of being deceiving; I am not deceiving, I am just made of silk. It is they who are stupid and wrongly take gentleness and fairness for weakness. There are many more predators in this world, so I want you to be made of silk. You are silk.

C. JoyBell C.

A coward is incapable of exhibiting love; it is the prerogative of the brave.

Mahatma Gandhi

Here are the values that I stand for: honesty, equality, kindness, compassion, treating people the way you want to be treated and helping those in need. To me, those are traditional values.

Ellen DeGeneres

It takes hands to build a house but only hearts can build a home

It is love that can save our world.

We are brothers and sisters so be good to others

Helping hands are better than praying lips

www.ingramcontent.com/pod-product-compliance
Lightning Source LLC
Chambersburg PA
CBHW031132250726
48655CB00002B/626